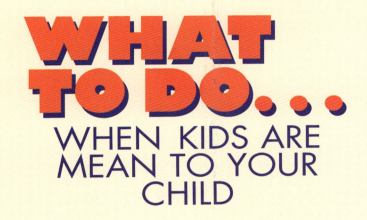

WHAT TO DO...

WHEN KIDS ARE MEAN TO YOUR CHILD

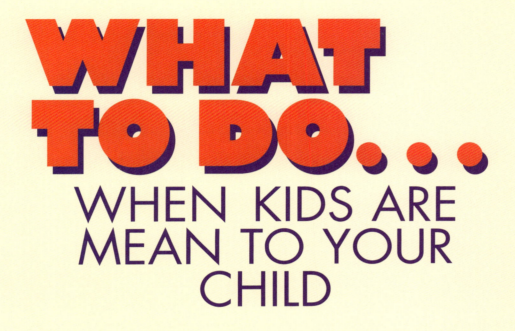

WHAT TO DO. . .
WHEN KIDS ARE MEAN TO YOUR CHILD

ELIN McCOY

Reader's Digest

The Reader's Digest Association, Inc.
Pleasantville, N.Y./Montreal

Acknowledgments

Many thanks to all the parents and children who shared their problems and solutions with me. In all cases, their names have been changed to protect their privacy.

Thanks also to the many teachers and psychologists who have talked with me, sent me their research papers, and/or whose books have added to my knowledge on this subject over the years, especially:

Dr. Steven Asher, Sheila Bernard, Dr. Thomas J. Berndt, Dr. Robert Cairns, Dr. Marjorie Castro, Dr. Kenneth Dodge, Gail Fisher, Tip Frank, Dr. Nathaniel Floyd, Dr. John Lochman, Don McConkey, Richard Mills, Dr. Anthony Pellegrini, Dr. David Perry, Dr. Dorothea Ross, Dr. Myrna B. Shure, Dr. Ronald Slaby, Dr. Ronald Stephens, and Dr. Kaoru Yamamoto.

As always, I am grateful to my husband, John, my son, Gavin, and my many cousins and their children, who have always been willing to talk about their own experiences.

A Reader's Digest Book

Conceived, written, and produced by Pen & Pencil Books.
Reader's Digest Parenting Guide Series creators:
Elin McCoy (editorial); Judy Speicher (design)
Copyright © 1997 by Pen & Pencil Books LLC
All rights reserved. Unauthorized reproduction, in any manner, is prohibited.

Cover photograph: David Young-Wolff/PhotoEdit
Photographs: 7 Lawrence Midgale, 13 Howard Grey/Tony Stone Images, 14 Jim Whitmer/FPG International, 17 Steven W. Jones/FPG International, 22 David Young-Wolff/Tony Stone Images, 25 John Terence Turner/FPG International, 28 Jeffrey Myers/FPG International, 32 Jack Montgomery/ Bruce Coleman, Inc., 35 Robert Kusel/Tony Stone Images, 36 Lawrence Migdale/Tony Stone Images, 39 Stephen Ogilvy/Bruce Coleman, Inc., 41 Scott Barrow/Scott Barrow, Inc., 42 Mike Malyszko/FPG International, 46 Scott Barrow/Scott Barrow, Inc., 49 Lori Adamski Peek/Tony Stone Images, 51 Arthur Tilley/FPG International, 62 Lawrence Migdale, 65 Wayne Eastep/Tony Stone Images, 66 Bruce Meyers/FPG International, 69 Scott Barrow/Scott Barrow, Inc., 72 Stewart Cohen/Tony Stone Images, 77 Arthur Tilley/FPG International, 78 Steven W. Jones/FPG International, 83 Stephen Simpson/FPG International, 87 Charles Thatcher/Tony Stone Images, 91 Paul Barton /The Stock Market.
Illustration: 61 Ray Skibinski.

Library of Congress Cataloging in Publication Data
McCoy, Elin
    What to do . . . when kids are mean to your child / Elin McCoy.
      p. cm. — (Reader's digest parenting guides)
    ISBN 0-89577-984-6
    1. Agressiveness (Psychology) in children.   2. Anger in children.   3. Child psychology.
4. Parenting. I. Title. II. Series.
BF723.A35M33   1997
649' .1—dc21   97-2464

Printed in the United States of America

CONTENTS

Between the ages of five and thirteen, our children spend most of their waking hours with other kids, both classmates and siblings, and as all parents know, the paths of these relationships are rarely smooth. Teasing, bullying, name-calling, rejection, and all sorts of mean behavior are part of growing up during the years when our kids are in elementary and middle school—and all these forms of meanness have a powerful impact on how they see themselves.

Have you heard one of these complaints from your child lately?

"Janie called me 'stinkpot.' She's not my friend anymore."

"Eric laughed at my sneakers. He says I'm totally out of it and can't be in his club."

"Allison didn't invite me to her Valentine party, but she invited every other girl in the eighth grade!"

"This older kid is always pushing me around on the playground."

For me, as for most parents, one of the hardest parts of parenting is seeing my child hurt by another child. Most of us don't know what to do and ask ourselves questions like these: Why are kids so mean to each other? Is this just part of how kids learn to get along? Should I get involved? How can I help my kid learn to handle the problem?

That's what this book is about.

The first section, **Real Stories & Situations**, is filled with stories of real children ages five to thirteen and the kinds of problems they've had with mean kids. In **Understanding The Problem**, you'll find answers to basic questions parents have about why and how kids engage in mean behavior and what effect it has on our kids. **What To Do** offers sound, practical solutions—actions that will help your children cope when others are mean. The fourth section, **Year By Year**, is a quick reference to how kids behave and the best solutions at different ages. **We Recommend** lists the best books and videos on the subject to share with your children and resources to further your own understanding.

REAL STORIES & SITUATIONS

Is One Of These Your Child's Story?

TOMMY, AGE 5

From his kitchen window, Tommy could see his friends Henry and Sam in Henry's huge sand pile in the backyard next door. They were having fun digging and dumping sand with their big plastic trucks and molding the piles into something that looked like a castle. Tommy hunted for his favorite red dump truck, then ran out the door to join them. "Can I play?" he asked uncertainly. "I have a truck, and I could help build the castle."

Henry and Sam were so busy they didn't even look up. "No, we don't want you," Henry said matter-of-factly. "Anyway, this is a fort, not a castle, and it's ours."

Sam looked at Tommy's truck and frowned. "We don't need a dump truck," he said. "We have excavators and you don't. So you can't play."

Tommy started to argue, then shouted, "You can't be mean! You didn't let me play yesterday so today you have to."

"No, we don't," Henry snapped. "You don't know how to build a good tunnel. This is our fort."

"Stop bothering us and go away. We don't want you for a friend anymore," Sam announced crossly.

Hugging his truck, his eyes filling with tears and with a crushed look on his face, Tommy ran home and told his mom how mean his friends were.

TAMARA, AGE 6

In Tamara's apartment building lives another girl her age—a bossy know-it-all named Amanda, who also happens to be Tamara's best friend right now. Though Tamara is quiet and a little shy, the two girls seem able to play happily together for hours.

Amanda usually decides what they'll play and when, and Tamara usually goes along with her ideas. Both like to dress up as princesses, but recently Amanda has invented a new game called "The Princess and the Maid." Whoever plays the princess can choose the fanciest dress, wear the aluminum foil crown and a sparkly necklace, and give orders to the maid. The maid has to wear something plain and ugly, like Amanda's mom's old brown dress that has no belt, and her duties include brushing the princess's hair fifty strokes, cleaning up, and addressing the princess as "Your Highness."

After cheerfully playing the maid, Tamara wants to be the princess. Her mom overhears the conversation. "You have to be the maid," Amanda insists. "I'm prettier and princesses are the pretty ones."

"I'm pretty, too!" protests Tamara.

"If you aren't the maid, I won't play," retorts Amanda. "And I won't invite you to my birthday party. You have to do what I say, or I'll let Katie be my best friend."

"You're so mean," Tamara cries. "I don't want to be the maid."

ALEX, AGE 7

Something is always happening to Alex, who is small for his age but also articulate, brainy, and well-liked for his good sense of humor. When he stepped off the school bus one crisp, fall day, blood was trickling from the corner of his puffy-lipped mouth, there were streaks of tears and dirt on his face, and his glasses were in two pieces.

On the bus, a mean kid named Cody had bashed him, Alex told his dad, and later, over dinner that night, the rest of the story about Cody came out. This wasn't the first time he had hurt Alex on the bus. Once he had thrown a partly eaten apple that hit Alex's head. Another time he had tripped Alex in the bus aisle, but then told the bus driver that Alex had deliberately kicked him.

Alex complained that Cody was always setting him up at school so he, not Cody, was the one who got into trouble. During recess, when the teacher wasn't looking, Cody punched or kicked Alex so he could

▶ PARENT TIPS

Check Your Own Reaction

▶ Tommy's mom made a big fuss, plied Tommy with cookies to make him—and herself—feel better, and spent the afternoon playing with him so he wouldn't have to be alone.
"Finally I realized why I was so upset," she says. "Tommy reminds me of myself when I was little—I was the youngest, too, and my older sisters were always telling me to go away, that I couldn't play. It dawned on me that my reaction wasn't going to help Tommy solve his problem. I needed to look at what was happening more objectively."

▶ Tamara's mom says, "I hate to admit it, but my first thought was, 'Why is Tamara such a doormat? Why doesn't she tell Amanda she'll get a new best friend?' Fortunately I didn't say it out loud. I was blaming Tamara instead of trying to show her how to talk back to Amanda."

▶ Alex's dad was so furious at Cody that he started shouting, "That kid is going to pay for your glasses. His parents are going to hear about this. Their kid needs a lecture on how to be a human being!"
"I was all set to be the avenging angel," he says. "Alex was so worried I'd make things worse for him that he tried to calm me down by excusing Cody, saying he probably didn't mean to do it. I realized I couldn't help him if I didn't calm myself down first."

get the ball or be first in line for the slide. Then when Alex hit back, Cody headed for the teacher and accused Alex of starting the fight. Alex told the teacher that Cody was the mean one who started it, but she didn't believe him.

GRACE, AGE 8

Grace, a cheerful and energetic third grader, got her first pair of glasses about two weeks after school started in September. Her mom and dad warned her that a few kids might tease her about them, but Grace wasn't worried. After all, when her older sister teased her because she liked to bite her toast into a tiny heart shape before swallowing it, she just didn't pay any attention, and her sister's teasing stopped.

Sure enough, the first day she wore her glasses to school, a tall boy in her class named Peter pointed a finger at her in the cafeteria and chanted in a loud sing-song, "Grace has four eyes, Grace has four eyes! She looks nerdy." Then his two buddies joined in, chortling, before they headed off to the lunchroom line.

"He's a mean jerk," said her friend Sandy sympathetically. "Don't pay any attention to him. Your new glasses look great. I wish I had glasses, too."

Grace did ignore Peter, but the next day he sauntered back and forth past the table in the cafeteria where she and her friends

sat, each time muttering under his breath, "You're a dork with four eyes, four eyes," then snickering.

By the end of the week Grace was really upset. She had tried responding, "You're counting wrong, I only have two," but her voice was trembling because she felt like crying. And it didn't stop Peter. Grace's friends had tried to help her. Sandy even told Peter her older brother would beat him up if he didn't leave her friend alone.

KATHERINE, AGE 9

Katherine's favorite activity of the week is her Saturday morning art class at the local community center. She is a better artist than most of the other kids and takes her work very seriously. So even though a group of her friends from fourth grade are in the class, Katherine usually chooses to sit by herself. She needs quiet to concentrate.

One Saturday Leah, a new fourth-grade girl who seems pretty nice, joins the class but has to leave early. Afterward, as she is cleaning up her paints, Katherine over-hears the other fourth-grade girls gossiping about Leah and calling her a nasty name because she is African-American. Katherine is upset but doesn't know what to do.

The following Saturday, Katherine over-hears her friends saying the same mean things in voices loud enough for Leah to hear. Katherine knows she should stick up for Leah but she's worried her friends will turn on her if she does. She doesn't want to lose all her friends.

That night she asks her mom if she's being mean by not helping Leah.

BRIAN, AGE 10

Lanky, dark-haired Brian, a fifth grader, was thrilled to be in middle school so he could finally play on a school soccer team and keep his things in a locker instead of a cubby. For the first month or so, enthusiasm for school, his teachers, his new friends, and the team reigned.

Then his attitude toward school began to change. In the morning he dawdled over breakfast and whined about feeling sick. "I don't want to be at school so early," he insisted. His math teacher sent home a warning note that Brian wasn't concentrating in class.

Actually, Brian was scared of the eighth grader whose locker was across the hall from his. Whenever he was there early and the hall was deserted, the eighth grader shoved him against the wall and warned in a deep, threatening voice, "You better watch it, kid. I'm gonna get you one of these days." Sometimes he said he'd beat Brian up on his way home after school.

Brian started carrying all his books for the day in his backpack so he wouldn't have to stop by his locker during the day.

Then one night the eighth grader called Brian at home and threatened, "I'll see you tomorrow morning on the way to school. You better be prepared to hand over a couple of dollars because I have a knife."

Brian's dad heard the threat because the speaker phone was on.

JEFF, AGE 11

Jeff has two brothers, thirteen and six, and a sister who is eight. His parents are dismayed by the way their four children pick on one another and trade insults. One summer they started building a skateboard ramp in the garage, and from the beginning, complaints began to flow, especially from Jeff.

His youngest brother called him "poopyhead," Jeff complained, then would giggle and hide in the bathroom when Jeff got mad. The eight-year-old sided with her younger brother against Jeff by periodically swiping the special comic books he kept by the toolbox and refusing to reveal where they were. His older brother, on the other hand, constantly criticized Jeff's abilities with disparaging and sarcastic remarks like, "Jeff, can't you pound nails in straight by now? You're always such a klutz! That's probably why you can't even do an ollie without falling."

"I have the meanest brothers and sister in the world," Jeff wailed to his parents.

ASK THE EXPERTS

According to several psychologists, there are 3 mistakes parents often make.

• **They don't take their child's complaint seriously.** It's hard enough just to admit to being hurt, rejected, or afraid. It's even harder if your parents don't sympathize and offer help.

• **They ask insensitive questions** like, "What did you do to make him hit you?" before they listen. This makes kids feel that what happened is their fault.

• **They take what is happening personally,** overreacting and blowing typical meanness out of proportion. If your child isn't invited to a birthday party, she isn't doomed to be a social failure forever.

DID YOU KNOW ?

◆ Mean behavior among kids is a universal problem. In a poll of 232 kids in kindergarten through 8th grade at a Connecticut elementary school, every child claimed to have been the victim of at least one schoolmate's or sibling's mean-ness in the previous month.

ANNA, AGE 12

In September two new kids—twin girls—joined Plainfield School's seventh grade. Within a couple of weeks they were part of the most popular group of girls, which also included Anna and her best friends since third grade, Sarah and Melanie. For a while they were always together. But one Monday morning in November, the four other girls ignored Anna when she arrived at school. Taped on her locker was a crumpled note. On it was scrawled, "You think you're so great, but you're not. We know your secret." It was signed: The Club.

For Anna, that day was a nightmare. When she tried to talk to the twins during homeroom, they pointedly turned away from her and started whispering. At lunch her friends told her she couldn't sit with them at their usual table, and said, "We don't want someone who does the things you do."

Anna found other girls to sit with but was too upset to talk to them because she could see her friends whispering and laughing, then slyly looking over at her.

That afternoon in the hall, when she walked by the group and two boys she sort of liked, they all snickered and called out, "We know your secret." One of the twins mimicked the way Anna flipped her long hair back with her hand, and all the others just laughed.

Anna felt awful. What had she done? She called Sarah after school to find out what it was and apologize, but Sarah said in a cold voice, "Don't call me again. I can't talk to you." Anna thought she could hear the twins giggling on the extension.

Soon she realized that the twins were spreading rumors about her. One girl let it slip that if any girl in the class talked to Anna, she couldn't be in the twins' group.

That night Anna's mother found her sobbing on her bed.

JASON, AGE 13

Jason had a problem in the boys' locker room before and after gym class. Two tough boys were grabbing other kids' clothes. Sometimes they just threw the clothes back and forth to each other, laughing while the owner tried to catch and retrieve them. Sometimes they stuffed them in an old bucket in the janitor's closet in the hall. When any kids complained, the two boys said, "Hey, don't get worked up! We're just joking around."

They asked Jason to join them and told him that if he didn't, he was their enemy and fair game. When he refused, they took his new tennis shoes and threw them in the toilet.

Jason's parents kept asking him why he didn't wear his new shoes. Finally, he had to admit what had happened. ❑

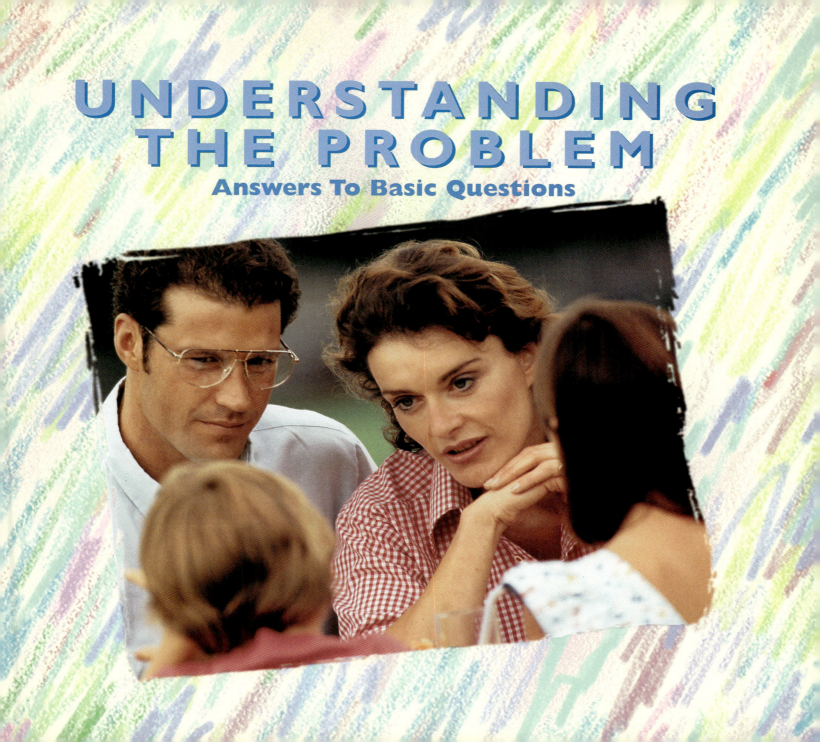

UNDERSTANDING THE PROBLEM
Answers To Basic Questions

What Does "Being Mean" Mean?

"Mom, Danny is being mean to me!" Is there a parent who hasn't heard a version of this universal kid complaint? In my house the phrase "being mean" has been applied to an amazingly wide range of behavior.

When my son was five, the meaning was often no more than "I want to play with the Etch-a-Sketch right now, and Danny won't give it to me." But through the years, "being mean" has meant everything from "Danny keeps calling me a dopey dork" to "At recess Danny hits me for no reason" to "Danny said he was my best friend but now he's started a club without me" to "Danny is always breaking promises."

Of course, the mean one wasn't always Danny; sometimes it was Alex or Charlie or Caroline or even, horrors, my own son.

Kids know what being mean is

Though "being mean" sounds like a vague concept, kids, just like adults, usually

have a very clear idea of what constitutes mean behavior. By grade school they regard it as deliberate, unfair, and intended to make them feel bad. That's what makes it mean. To children, all mean behavior, whatever its form, is interrelated; it's just a matter of degree. Some kids do recognize, though, that maybe, just maybe, the person who's been mean didn't realize what he was doing and made a mistake.

Parents often hear about other kids' meanness and are highly aware just how much it results in their own kids feeling sad, hurt, disappointed, and angry, and how it affects their self-image in a negative way. What I remind myself is that no one gets through childhood—or life—without experiencing others' meanness on the playground, in the classroom, in friendships, and with siblings. If we can understand the ways in which kids are mean and why, we can begin to know how to help our children develop the skills they need to handle these problems successfully on their own. The most common ways kids are mean to one another fall into several categories.

Rejecting and excluding

By far the most prevalent type of meanness occurs when kids exclude or reject another child. Two of your child's friends are playing or talking, and they tell your child he can't join in. But there are many other ways to let kids know they're not wanted:

"You can't sit here." "Don't follow us." "I'm only telling Jill the secret, not you." "I don't want you to be my partner." "We already have enough people in our group."

Not being invited to a birthday party is a big source of hurt feelings in elementary school, as is being chosen last for a team. Children of all ages remember these rejections with surprising intensity.

Teasing, name-calling, and put-downs

Even at a young age children can usually distinguish between playful teasing or making silly faces with a friend and the hurtful teasing that pokes fun to make people feel bad, which can involve either words or actions. First and second graders often resort to physical teasing, like grabbing someone's hat, tossing it back and forth, and refusing to give it back.

Name-calling is one form of verbal teasing, and usually it targets something negative about a person, such as weight or size, as in "Big Butt," "Fatso," "Shrimp," "Peewee," and "the Nose." No matter what the children's ages or whether they are boys or girls, these words hurt, and the impact they have lasts. Other names insult someone's intelligence or personality, as in "dummy" and "sissy," and still others are racial and ethnic slurs, which have a special ugliness. Put-downs and casual insults usually incorporate sarcasm and call attention to an individual's shortcomings.

Harassing about sex

Sexual teasing, both verbal and physical, is as common in middle school as it always has been, and overwhelmingly boys are the ones who do it, targeting both girls and other boys. Some of it is a playful and acceptable way of dealing with emerging sexual feelings. But all too often the forms it takes cross a boundary of respect, becoming insulting and aggressive. Snapping a girl's bra strap, making fun of someone's body in the locker room, grabbing a girl's breast, or pinching her bottom are all examples of this.

Humiliating and embarrassing

In my son's second grade were two children noted for playing tricks and doing things to others that embarrassed and humiliated them. They pulled up girls' skirts on the playground, calling attention to the color of their underpants. They pinned a note on someone's back that read "I'm stupid," and they put a dead cockroach under a girl's peanut butter sandwich and laughed when she screamed. Of course, this kind of behavior is not limited to second grade.

Gossiping and spreading rumors

Girls, especially those ages eight and up, are particularly adept at these underhanded forms of meanness that are similar to name-calling but more indirect. By gossiping behind someone's back, they can be mean while still pretending to be nice and actually avoid confronting the person.

Breaking basic rules of friendship

Throughout elementary school kids are learning what a friend is and how to be one. By age nine, they generally have clear expectations of how their friends should behave. Not living up to those expectations—by breaking promises, blabbing a friend's secret to someone else, or even confiding something important to another child—is definitely considered mean.

Intimidating through threats

"If you won't do what I say, I won't be your friend" is one of those mild threats that cause fear and anxiety even in five-year-olds. As kids get older, threats can take a much more ominous turn and include everything from "You better watch it!" to "I'll beat up your sister if you don't let me copy your paper."

Getting physical

Physical meanness is obvious. It starts with the pushing, shoving, spitting, and hitting typical of younger kids and becomes more serious when children get older. Tripping someone, locking someone in a closet, destroying a backpack, breaking glasses, or beating someone up are recognized by kids as the ultimate mean behavior. ❑

On a day when your children and their friends are behaving badly to one another you can't help but ask yourself, "Is it human nature to be cruel? Why do kids act this way?"

Most children aren't heartless, cruel, or unfeeling, nor are they going around looking for someone to be mean to. If you look underneath the surface of mean behavior, you can usually find a reason for it, at least from a kid's point of view.

When they can't solve a conflict

Two kids and one toy or TV or cookie is almost always a recipe for conflict. Both children want something, and only one can have it. Usually the result is a fight. Depending on the individuals and their ages, this means a few slaps at each other or some choice mean remarks: "You're so fat you shouldn't have a cookie," for example. The purpose is not really to hurt the other person, but to get what you want.

If these kids stop, though, and figure out how to solve the real problem instead of just reacting immediately, they probably won't feel the need to be mean to each other. Even five-year-olds can learn to work through conflicts.

When they're angry or frustrated

Seven-year-old Kevin was furious at his little brother Joe for knocking down his block building, so he ran for the red poster paint and poured it on Joe's favorite teddy bear. Joe cried. When their mom told Kevin his action had made Joe very upset, he said, "Good. I wanted it to." Like many kids who do something mean, Kevin was angry and wanted to retaliate. This desire to strike back at someone who has hurt you is one of the most common causes of mean behavior.

If Kevin could learn other, more appropriate ways to express his anger, he might not feel the need to be mean.

When there are no rules

Children in the five-to-thirteen age group are learning to respect rules. Since they don't always know how to behave appropriately, they rely on guidance from adults to help them know what to do. Mean behavior is always more common where there are no clear rules.

17

► PARENT TIPS

► "Sometimes a kid acts 'mean' because he's a victim somewhere else," reports Angela, mother of 2. "Every day when he came home from school, my 10-year-old, Isaac, started pounding on his 7-year-old sister. I couldn't understand it! They had always been such friends!

"It turned out that two boys in the 7th grade were picking on Isaac right after school. He felt humiliated and powerless. I realized he was trying to regain his dignity. Hitting his sister let him feel that he was still important and powerful."

"Be nice to each other" isn't as specific or effective as rules like "no hitting" or "name-calling, teasing, and making fun of someone are absolutely not allowed."

A matter of age and development

Some reasons for meanness vary with age and stages of social development. At ages five, six, and seven, kids are primarily self-centered. Often they don't realize how their words or actions affect someone else because they haven't yet learned how to look at things from another's point of view.

Girls and boys ages seven to ten know the basics of friendship, and their mean gossip, snubs, teasing, and fights are often ways of testing just how far they can go and still stay friends.

Between the ages of nine and thirteen kids generally have a great need to be part of a group, and the desire to fit in leads them to do cruel things in a misguided attempt to belong. Making humorous but cutting remarks directed at an outsider is an easy way to win admiration and define just who's in the group and who is not. Jealousy is yet another motive.

When they have emotional problems

Kids who act tough and aggressive, bullying others regularly, often are having problems at home. For instance, if a child's parents are getting divorced, he may play out his own worries by striking out. Other aggressive kids may have parents who punish them harshly or encourage them to act in a "macho" way, or have older siblings who push them around.

The power of role models

We all recognize how quick children are to copy what they see and hear, and there are plenty of mean-spirited role models in today's society. Just consider what appears on TV on an average evening: violence and brutality, politicians putting one another down, sarcastic remarks accompanied by a laughtrack, and cartoons in which the entire script is one mean remark or action after another.

If, in addition, teachers make sarcastic remarks to students, and older siblings regularly tease and make fun of younger ones, it's no wonder some children get the idea that they have a right to be mean, too. ❑

Most of us recall how loud the voices of rejection and exclusion seemed in elementary and middle school. Wanting to develop friendships with kids who are like you is natural, but does someone always have to be shut out?

It's developmental

Sometimes exclusion results more from children's limited social skills than from deliberate meanness. Whenever my son at age six had two friends over, two of the three would end up refusing to let the third play. My son was relieved when I laid down a "no threesomes" rule. Like many young kids, he didn't know how to pay attention to two friends at once.

The power of jealousy

Wanting to keep a friend or several friends all to yourself and being worried you'll lose them are powerful motives for children to reject others. The web of exclusive friendships among seven- to ten-year-old girls is rife with intense jealousy, rivalry, and constant rejection. Best friends are ousted and replaced. Third-grader Bethany, for example, chooses Melissa, a new girl, to be her best friend instead of Sonya because Sonya talks to Dawn at recess. Two girls won't share a secret with a third, or they refuse to play with her after school. The next day the alliance shifts, and a different girl finds herself excluded.

Defining in and out

Rejection also occurs when kids form groups and view everyone else, especially someone who looks or acts different, as an outsider. Having a particular skill may be necessary to be included in some groups. For eight-year-old Jason, being part of an exclusive bunch of boys who play computer games after school helps him define the kind of person he is. The cliques of middle school are a version of this (see pages 24-27), as are gangs.

Children may have problems with rejection if they're not like other kids at their school. A nine-year-old "brain" who has been excluded in the past may suddenly become popular when he enters a competitive school for gifted kids.

Kids that aren't liked

We've all seen how judgmental our children can be. When kids are left out a lot, it may be because they are doing something very specific that turns other kids off. In grade school, no one wants to play with children who hit and kick, or who are bossy and disruptive. But kids also single out others who are socially inept or indulge in behavior more appropriate to younger kids, such as not playing by the rules and arguing about it.

Then there are the difficult cases of kids who are locked into a pattern or habit of being rejected (see pages 36-38). ❑

Why Do Kids Exclude Others?

Why Do Kids Tease & Call Names?

Even in the best schools, the most caring families, and the ideal neighborhoods, teasing and name-calling are two universal problems kids face during the elementary-school years. It's an experience they dread. Annie, a ten-year-old, looks at herself in the bathroom mirror every morning and calls herself "ugly witch" and "big, fat whale" to practice not reacting to the names she knows she'll hear from another girl at school.

A desire for power over someone else is the primary reason for name-calling and teasing. Older siblings frequently experiment on their younger siblings with a number of different names and techniques so they can feel older and superior.

A new, sophisticated skill

For five- and six-year-olds, teasing and name-calling also reflect their growing ability to use words. When you think about it, teasing is certainly a more advanced skill in dealing with others than hitting is— a fact kids recognize. One boy I know unmercifully teases his little brother. When his mother intervenes, he says proudly, "But Mom, I didn't smack him! I used words—just the way you said I had to!"

Teasing and making ugly faces allow children to have a very satisfying and dramatic effect on others without resorting to physical violence.

A lack of empathy

Starting around the age of six, children begin to understand how remarks and the way they're delivered make people feel, but until about age ten they don't completely grasp the degree of emotional impact their harsh words can have. Ray, who had a slight speech defect in elementary school, was called "retard" by the boys in his third-grade class. Twenty years later he can still remember the sting of that word.

Testing the limits

If your kids are like most, they're always testing limits. Between the ages of five and thirteen, kids experiment to find out what's acceptable in friendship. Since they see that teasing, calling names, and making faces are sometimes considered okay, they wonder: "Where does the boundary for what's acceptable lie?" "How far can I go before friends get upset?" Usually the "insults" applied to friends must be false

▶ PARENT TIPS

▶ "To help my son cope with teasing, we played a regular nightly teasing game. We'd take turns saying completely silly and really gross things about each other. He loved dreaming up these comebacks and finally was able to use a couple on the kid who teased him at school," says his dad, Richard.

and exaggerated in order not to be hurtful. You can call a friend an "idiot," but you can't call her a "fat slug" if she really is fat. In one study, fifth graders were more likely than third graders to see teasing as fun.

Teasers learn to gauge just how far they can go. I've watched siblings push and push, then stop just as their victim is about to get upset, but often teasing stops only when someone says, "If you do that just one more time, I'll get you" or "I'll tell."

Because of insecurity or jealousy

Kids also tease and name call because they feel insecure or jealous of another child. By ridiculing someone else, they make themselves feel more confident and superior—and if the name is hilarious enough, it wins them attention and admiration from other children.

To define their social group

A new sixth grader, Lauren, wears old-fashioned skirts and hair ribbons to school. A bunch of girls who wear the latest styles have been teasing her about her clothes and calling her "an immature little school-girl." One reason why kids tease and put down others in this way is to define their own group, by directing gibes at kids who look different. When boys tease in middle school, they often target one another's masculinity. By early adolescence, though, the prevalence of mean teasing starts to fade.

ASK THE EXPERTS

Dr. Theodore R. Warm, a child psychiatrist in Cleveland, Ohio, asked 250 children and adolescents about teasing.

• **Eighty percent reported that they liked to tease to make someone else miserable. Only 20% engaged in teasing with a friendly intent.**
• **Most kids said they coped with teasing on their own. Of the 1st graders, 25% said they told a parent or teacher, but by 3rd grade only 10% did.**
• **Kids typically go through stages in teasing. First graders engage in physically hurtful teasing, like tying a classmate's shoes together. By 6th grade kids use "mean" teasing, such as calling an unattractive girl "ugly."**

Because of a teacher

Sometimes a teacher sets a child up for teasing. Robert's teacher was always calling attention to his daydreaming in a negative and sarcastic way, as in "Well, Robert, when you come down from the clouds, could you collect the papers?" Before long, the children in the class picked up her lead and started teasing him regularly about being from "outer space." ❑

Is Hitting Just A Phase All Kids Go Through?

The third-grade teacher telephoned Nick's mother to tell her that her son was in trouble again, this time for kicking another boy and jabbing him in the stomach with his elbow so hard that the boy had to go to the school nurse. Nick told his mom, "I had to kick Alexander, Mom! He wasn't going to let me in the game." Nick's mom was worried about his belligerent attitude but secretly she thought: Hitting is mean, but it's probably just typical boy behavior Nick will grow out of eventually—but how soon?

When kids stop hitting

Boys do hit more than girls, but this kind of physically aggressive behavior usually diminishes with age. Slapping, grabbing, hitting, even biting are part of the territory with rambunctious two- and three-year-olds of either gender. Some, especially boys, are more impulsive and excitable and hit more than others to express anger or get what they want.

This method of dealing with others is established early, researchers have discovered, and often will continue if

DID YOU KNOW?

◆ Research has shown that in many cultures, boys between the ages of 5 and 11 are more likely than girls to engage in active play in large groups—anything from harmless pranks to competitive games to gangs. The hierarchy within the group is important to them.

not stopped. It's one type of mean behavior that most parents and preschools forbid and punish. As a result, most children learn that they'll get in trouble if they're caught hitting hard.

In kindergarten and first grade, some boys still hit and these behave better in social situations when an adult is present than in unsupervised play. By second and third grade, the situation usually changes. The majority have learned more self-control and rely increasingly on negotiation and compromise to settle disagreements (although they may still resort to a punch occasionally). The few who still use force have become even more aggressive—now they're the bullies other children avoid.

Kids who are still using physical aggression by middle-school age have a definite and sometimes serious problem. Unless they get the proper psychological help, they are liable to get into more and more trouble as the years progress.

How kids feel about kids who hit

Kids who hit a lot are usually the least liked in the school or neighborhood. Some, like Nick, hurt others because they have a short fuse; when they feel attacked or threatened, they strike out before they consider the consequences. Kids who are hyperactive have a particular problem controlling their impulses in such situations. Those who, by the age of nine, are stuck in the mode of hitting to get what they want are the most disliked kids in their class.

Play fighting and mean fighting

Most of the fighting, chasing, hitting, and wrestling that about eighty percent of boys engage in from preschool to middle school isn't mean and aggressive behavior. Experts call it rough-and-tumble play. According to Dr. Anthony Pellegrini, a professor of early childhood education at the University of Georgia, "This type of play is one way that children, especially boys, learn social skills like negotiation. It continues throughout the primary grades. By middle school, though, it's only important to bands of anti-social boys."

Like many parents, I often have a hard time telling the difference between the two—and so do some boys. Here are a few differences. In real fights, kids look angry, grab one another fiercely, and strike with clenched fists. In rough-and-tumble play, kids hit only with open hands. Blows aren't actually intended to connect, and kids smile and laugh. Roles change often: the captured boys are soon the ones doing the capturing. Mean hitting usually involves disputes over toys and possessions, but rough-and-tumble play doesn't.

Boys who constantly confuse the two end up punching someone hard, turning a play fight into a real one, and don't understand why they get into trouble. ❑

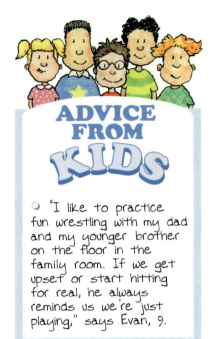

ADVICE FROM KIDS

○ "I like to practice fun wrestling with my dad and my younger brother on the floor in the family room. If we get upset or start hitting for real, he always reminds us we're just playing," says Evan, 9.

Why Do Cliques Exist?

Cliques are as prevalent today as they were when we were young—and just as painful for those who find themselves "out" instead of "in." They're easy to spot in any middle or junior high school. In one school, for example, anyone could pick out the tight-knit group of five popular and pretty sixth-grade girls—Anna, Julia, Becky, Christina, and Katie—sitting together at the center table in the lunchroom: they are all wearing red sweaters, grey felt clogs, black fingernail polish, and black velvet ribbons around their wrists, and their hair is in French braids.

Clearly these girls spent hours on the telephone the night before organizing this demonstration of solidarity, just as my friends and I used to. Their conversation is sprinkled with their special slang expression, "simply the best," frequent references to their favorite rock group, and dogmatic statements about the importance of being a vegetarian. Of course, they also agree on the ways several of their classmates don't measure up to their standards.

The constant in clique behavior

Though "in" group hair styles, clothing, music, and slang differ from group to group and school to school—it was straight hair and bangs, kilts, "cool," and the Beatles in my day—behavior toward outsiders is universal. "You can't sit here," these girls may say in a mocking tone when some-one pulls out a chair at their lunch table. "We're talking." During recess they gather at Julia's locker to whisper secrets and laugh, then suddenly huddle into a circle with their backs turned if certain girls venture to join them. This year one of the excluded girls is Jessica, the smartest girl in the class, who desperately wants to belong to their group.

Not surprisingly, their rejection makes her feel miserably unhappy. Much of their meanness to her—and others—consists in keeping her from joining the group and gossiping unkindly about why she wouldn't fit in. That's what a clique is all about. If anyone can belong, what's the point?

A matter of age

Ages eleven to thirteen, roughly grades six through eight, are when both boys and girls begin forming the cliques and secret clubs that often become powerful forces in their lives. The loose networks of friendships in earlier grades that changed almost daily give way to clearly defined social groups that are recognized by everyone at school. Jessica, like most kids, can describe precisely who's in each group and where each one fits in the junior-high social hierarchy. The "top" groups, like Julia's, are composed of the most popular kids; at the bottom are the "losers" that nobody else wants—kids who get into trouble, who hit and bully, who join gangs, and who cut school.

New rules of friendship

Most of us don't have to dig down very deep to remember how hard and confusing living through those years was. The rules of friendship suddenly seemed more complicated. It's the same today. Sharing a passion for playing video games is no longer a sufficient reason to be friends.

In middle school both boys and girls become more sophisticated about picking friends whose personalities as well as interests and values are a good match with theirs. They compare and exclude, and look to their friends to provide some of the sense of belonging and acceptance, guidance, and advice they used to seek only from their families. Why? Kids are ready, at this age, to edge away from home socially and begin identifying with their own generation.

ADVICE FROM KIDS

○ "Don't try to be part of a group that doesn't want you. Find one that doesn't have too many kids and likes you the way you are," says Justin, 11.

○ "Start your own clique. Think of what you're really interested in, like horses or writing stories. Then get other kids who like the same things to join with you," advises Miranda, 13.

○ "If a group doesn't want you it's not the end of the world," says Emma, 12. "Just pretend you don't care."

ASK THE EXPERTS

Dr. Thomas J. Berndt, a psychologist at Purdue University and an expert in children's friendships, points out 4 ways boys' and girls' cliques differ:

- **Girls are more exclusive. If a girl makes a bid to join a well-established group that already has 4 girls, they will probably reject her bid. In the same sized group, boys are more likely to accept another who wants to join.**
- **Girls express much more worry about being excluded and about others' faithfulness to the group.**
- **Because girls spend more time with a single friend within the group, jealousy and rivalry are more likely to arise in girls' cliques.**
- **Both boys and girls gossip, but girls focus more on telling private thoughts and feelings.**

An experimental family

When you think about it, cliques have a lot in common with families and offer some of the same kind of security. Like a family, they're small, usually just three to six members. Also like a family, kids in a clique spend a lot of time together. I remember sleepovers every weekend during which we confided secret fears and dreams and hanging out every afternoon in one special corner of the park.

By being part of a tight-knit, intimate group, kids know their social life is set: they'll always have someone to go to the movies with and sit with at lunch.

And, as Christina told me, "with your group you know you have somebody to talk to about what's bothering you and to help you decide what to think and do."

Pressure to conform

To many parents' dismay, kids in a clique generally pressure each other to become even more similar. Katie used to put her hair in a ponytail, but now she wears it in a French braid because Julia, Anna, Becky, and Christina want everyone to look alike. They've also made a pact that no one in their group will smoke, ever, even if they are tempted.

All this conformity to the group's standards is another way for kids to feel secure about some of their newfound opinions. It also helps them define exactly who's in and who's out and why. These rigid definitions are frequently asserted in cruel and hurtful ways because of kids' social inexperience. Generally, all the members in a clique agree upon how much and what kind of mean behavior to outsiders is acceptable. That's why the meanest and most dangerous kids end up together.

What about gossip?

We all cringe at the mean-spirited way our children talk about those outside their group. Julia's mom overheard this exchange:

"Jessica's smart, but she's a snot. I can't stand the way she acts so superior."

"She brags, too. She told Katie how fabulously she did on the math test when she knew that Katie practically failed."

"Last week she did the same thing to me! None of us would do that!"

But gossip is not all bad, according to one researcher on children's friendships, Dr. Thomas J. Berndt, who says, "Kids in a group use gossip to cement the ties and strengthen the bonds among them. Their negative put-downs are mostly a way of stating what their own standards are."

Why cliques aren't forever

Cliques usually don't last very long. Jealousies arise, loyalties shift, and in a short while kids may discover they have less in common than they thought.

The rapid physical and emotional changes kids go through in middle school are another reason groups change after a few months, as Sam's did in eighth grade. His best friend grew four inches, joined the basketball team, and abandoned Sam and his close friends for a more popular group of very athletic boys. Another member started smoking and drifted into a group that took risks. Sam and the other boys discovered they loved computers and banded together with a new boy who was a computer whiz.

Though even two weeks seems endless to preteens, especially when they are the ones rejected, Jessica and other excluded kids can take heart from the fact that their problem is usually temporary. Unless a school is very small, a clique rarely holds together for an entire year.

What kids can learn from cliques

Despite the "mean" aspect of exclusivity that parents—and their children—find so upsetting, cliques do help kids make sense of the social order of the school and figure out where they fit in.

Anna, Julia, Christina, Becky, Katie, and Jessica—and our own children—are learning lessons about the exclusive nature of friendship, one of which is that you can't share your private thoughts with everybody. Their clique is giving them experience and practice with the biggest problems of social life: How does it feel to be included or excluded? How much are you willing to conform? What are loyalty and betrayal? Why do friendships end?

Our big job as parents is to help children realize they can find new friends or a new group when the one they've been a part of hurts or disappoints them (see pages 50-53). ❑

(see pages 50-53).

DID YOU KNOW ?

◆ Frequently girls in a clique will suddenly single out the most popular member to exclude and attack, but not the one who is least popular. So say developmental psychologists Robert and Beverley Cairns, who have studied children's social networks for over 30 years.

When Is "Being Mean" Bullying?

My friend's son, Ben, has vivid and awful memories of fourth grade. That was the year the sixth-grade bully, Skipper, and his three pals decided that thin, super-smart Ben and a couple of his fourth-grade friends were ideal targets. On the playground they'd edge up close and lean over Ben, hulking up their shoulders and moving their arms as though they were just about to haul off and sock him.

Then Skipper would demand that Ben turn over his lunch money, push Ben around a little, scornfully spit on his shoes, and laugh as he fell against the fence and tore his shirt.

The way Skipper swaggered off told other kids, "Try messing with me and you're history." He and his buddies terrorized Ben and other boys on the playground for several months—until Skipper broke a second grader's nose at the beginning of

December, and the teachers discovered what was going on.

That was three years ago, but Ben, like most kids who have been bullied, can recall the smallest details of those daily encounters, especially his own feelings of helplessness and humiliation.

Unfortunately, bullying is a much bigger and more serious "meanness" problem than most parents and teachers think. Most experts estimate that at least one in ten— and probably more—kids in elementary and junior high school are bullied every year. Ben's story is all too common.

A definition of bullying

Sometimes it's hard for any parent to figure out where ordinary meanness ends and bullying begins. Ben's dad, like many parents, believed fighting off a bully was just another childhood rite of passage, a problem of "boys being boys." But now we know it's not just typical mean behavior.

When trying to distinguish the two, it helps to think of a continuum. At one end are those mildly nasty, but pretty typical, behaviors like pushing and shoving, name-calling, teasing, and telling someone you don't want them on your team. At the other end are activities that border on the criminal: slamming someone into a locker, extorting a toy, a lunch, a favorite jacket, or even money, and threatening kids with total isolation from everyone in the class.

Somewhere in the middle of this continuum, when one child or a group regularly torments another child psychologically or physically, the way Skipper and his friends did, typical childhood "meanness" becomes bullying. The kid who is picked on is someone who can't defend himself because he's smaller, younger, less socially savvy, or just a loner. But even relatively mild teasing becomes bullying if a more powerful kid picks on a weaker one over and over until he is distraught.

Psychological bullying such as ostracism is less conspicuous, but it can create as much fear and anxiety.

A typical bully

A bully is not just a mean child who likes to tease. He—or she—turns out to have a particular kind of personality. Dr. John Lochman, a psychologist at Duke University who has studied and worked with bullies for years, describes them as "children who have a strong need to control and dominate others, who enjoy having power over them and are willing to use force and intimidation to get their own way."

Another characteristic of bullies is the way they revel in the imbalance of power. Like Skipper, they seem to thrive on their victim's distress, as though that's what they're really after, and to find a victim's obedience more important than whatever they've extorted, whether possessions or

AGE FACTOR

❖ There are bullies in all schools and all grades, but one study showed that kids in the 2nd through the 6th grade are bullied twice as much as older kids, frequently by kids 1 or 2 years older than they are.

❖ In 1st and 2nd grade popular boys tend to bully to establish their place. But by 3rd and 4th grade this kind of behavior isn't acceptable, and the boys who are less popular become the bullies.

DID YOU KNOW ?

Six facts about bullying most parents don't know:

◆ Parents of both victims and bullies are usually unaware of the problem because most victims don't report it.

◆ Bullies have pals who join in, but victims usually become isolated.

◆ Many teachers and schools do not talk about bullying or try to stop it.

◆ Girls and boys are verbal bullies in almost equal numbers.

◆ Most bullies pick on more than one child at a time.

◆ Most victims are bullied by different children at different times.

some action. The bullies I've known didn't have empathy for anyone, could not care less how much another child was hurt, and never seemed to feel the slightest guilt over what they'd done.

A recent study from the Center for Adolescent Studies at Indiana University found that bullies also generally spend less time with adults, watch more violent television, and misbehave at home more than other kids.

Like many people, I used to think of bullies as big, dumb, unhappy loners who were insecure. But bullies tend to be strong and confident, average to just below average in intelligence and school achievement, and believe violence is an acceptable way to solve problems. At younger ages they are often popular and admired as well as feared, but as time goes on their popularity fades. Nevertheless, they continue to have friends who admire and encourage them and who gain status from the relationship, just the way Skipper's friends did.

The difference between boys and girls

Even though boys account for eighty percent of physical bullying, girls can be bullies too, a fact I've known since fifth grade. My classmate Peggy convinced most of the class that one girl had "cooties" and that we'd catch them if we sat next to her and be outcasts, too. For several weeks that girl had no one to sit or play with.

Boys more readily admit to being bullies than girls. Within a few weeks of the start of school, kids know who the boy bullies are because the tactics they use are physical and obvious. They're much more likely than girls to beat someone up or threaten to do so, and they frequently pick on girls as well as boys. Girl bullies, like Peggy, are usually more insidious and psychologically manipulative, and almost always bully other girls. After the age of ten they rarely employ the overt tactics that boys do. Instead they use threats of social ostracism, the way Peggy did, or spread malicious rumors or send intimidating notes.

Boys and girls are equally likely to extort possessions or money, sometimes by promising victims they'll be included in a special group if they pay up.

Where bullying occurs

The truth is that teachers and parents don't see most bullying situations. At Ben's school, for example, the bullies were out in force whenever and wherever adults were not around to supervise closely.

The playground is the major locale, along with the girls' and boys' bathrooms, deserted hallways, cafeteria, and locker rooms. My son and his friends, like many kids, encountered a bully in another favored place: the school bus. Bullies also sometimes lie in wait for kids walking to and from school.

Some schools have a bigger bullying problem than others, but the size of the school doesn't matter. What counts is whether there is adequate supervision and whether the school creates an atmosphere and establishes rules that actively discourage bullying. Many schools do not.

What about bystanders?

The majority of kids, who are neither bullies nor victims, don't usually come to a victim's aid, even though many don't approve of bullying. Often they try to ignore what's happening, afraid that if they get involved they'll be the next target. Some feel upset with themselves for not helping, while others blame the victim. The lack of adult rules against bullying makes them feel vulnerable, too, and they think: This could happen to me.

A problem with serious consequences

When you consider how upset your children can be after they've been left out of a game at recess, you can easily imagine how kids who are bullied feel. They become unhappy and depressed, anxious and insecure, and develop low opinions of themselves. As a result, they find it difficult to concentrate on their schoolwork and often begin withdrawing from activities with other kids. In a few extreme cases, after being bullied for as much as several years, children in middle school have actually brought guns to school and shot their tormentors or committed suicide in despair.

Conventional wisdom has it that if kids just punch a bully back, he'll stop. Despite the many stories you read about boys who finally manage to beat the bully up, this doesn't happen as much in real life as it does in books or movies—and today, when more and more students bring weapons to school, it's dangerous advice.

Though many parents believe that bullying is a phase, all experts agree that this is not true. Without adult intervention, it continues, and the bullies and victims rarely get the help they need (see page 86). ❑

ASK THE EXPERTS

• "Many bullies see the world with a paranoid's eye," observes Dr. Kenneth Dodge, a psychologist at Vanderbilt University. "They see threats where none exist, and they take these imagined threats as provocation to strike back. They feel justified in retaliating for what are actually imaginary harms."

In other words, if your son accidentally spills a lunch tray on a bully, the bully will lash out at your son because he'll assume your son did it on purpose.

Do All Kids React The Same Way?

The short answer is no, kids don't all react the same way to mean behavior, just as they don't all react the same way to going to bed at a particular time, parental discipline, school requirements, or what's being served for dinner.

Take the three children in the Thompson family. The oldest, Jerry, is twelve. He's tall, athletic, cheerful, calm, and fairly oblivious to mean behavior of any kind. He tends to brush it off even when one of his siblings is trying hard to "push his buttons." The youngest, Kathleen, is seven, vociferous about being treated unfairly and quick with a comeback when her brothers or other kids tease. She becomes tremendously upset if she feels slighted or rejected by one of her friends and complains regularly that no one likes her. The middle one, Nathaniel, is ten. Moody, emotional, hyper-sensitive, and hot-tempered, he's the one who ends up in the center of any fray in the backyard, at school, at the ballfield, and at practically every large family gathering.

As parents we have to recognize that not all kids have the same sensitivity to what others say and do.

A question of temperament

Experts now believe that a child's basic temperament is inherited, a result of the neurological wiring in his brain. When helping children deal with mean kids, we have to take their temperaments into account. If your kids are usually even-tempered, not overly sensitive, outgoing, and flexible, they probably take most ordinary mean behavior in stride. Alas, a great many children are not like this.

Joanne, who is moody and pessimistic, expects the worst and on some days goes into a funk if anyone looks cross-eyed at her. Her parents now try to help her recognize how her mood is related to the way she reacts to others' actions.

Eric is supersensitive to every nuance of what kids say and do. That makes him very sympathetic and caring to others, but it's also easy for them to hurt his feelings. His parents are trying to help him develop a thicker skin.

Timid Barbara is thrown by new situations or big groups. Like the fifteen to twenty percent of children who are shy, she easily becomes anxious and fearful, especially around classmates. When anyone teases or becomes bossy, she seems to shrink into herself and tries to become invisible. Then, when others ignore her, she wonders why everyone leaves her out. Her parents are helping her become more confident and comfortable with others

by inviting one child over at a time and encouraging her gift for drawing through a small art class.

Some children are both shy and aggressive (an unusual combination), and these kids often become either bullies or victims and sometimes both.

We all know hot-tempered, impulsive children who can't seem to count to ten before they act. They frequently overreact when someone is mean to them by lashing out to retaliate and end up getting in trouble themselves. Their parents need to help them practice anticipating situations where they "lose it" and controlling their emotions better (see pages 54-55).

Kids who are forceful and intense, who have trouble switching from one thing to

> ▶ **PARENT TIPS**

> ▶ "Don't assume that a shy child is feeling rejected because she only has one friend. The number of friends a child has ranges greatly from child to child. Be sure you're not worried because you wish your child were more popular," advises Lisa, mother of a shy 10-year-old.

> ▶ "Don't tell your child he is too sensitive or just a crybaby if he complains that others are picking on him. That will just make him feel guilty for feeling hurt and angry, and he'll feel even more inadequate. And he'll be less likely to tell you because he'll be afraid of losing your acceptance and affection," says Bob, father of a 6-year-old boy.

another, who are picky, demanding, easily stimulated, and stubborn react more strongly to other kids' meanness, and often do and say things that keep that behavior coming (see pages 54-55).

Research by Jerome Kagan at Harvard University suggests that inborn differences in neural circuitry may make shy, super-sensitive, and excitable children less able to tolerate stress than others do. To them, the teasing, bullying, or rejection that others simply take in stride may seem so stressful that they have trouble coping.

The difference between boys and girls

Girls have more exclusive, intense, and intimate friendships than boys do, worry more about being left out or losing a friend, and may react to rejection and teasing in more obvious, emotional ways. Many studies in the past twenty years have shown this, and most parents who have both girls and boys would probably agree.

By the beginning of middle school, girls are highly self-conscious and describe themselves as easier to hurt than boys, especially when it comes to teasing about their looks, weight, figures, and clothes. Boys seem more able to take an independent stance in terms of being in or out of a group—"So what if they don't like me?"—but they are also more likely to feel called upon to defend themselves physically to prove they are not "sissies."

How kids explain what's happening

Why is it that one child who is left out of a sleepover party sulks in her room for days and is wary of trying to be part of the group again, while another child bounces back from rejection easily?

Many psychologists believe part of the difference has to do with the way children explain rejection to themselves. Some children, like Kathleen, who takes every little rebuff to heart, blame their own inadequacies. "I'm not that good at games. That's why no one really likes me," they'll say. These kids may need help to boost their self-esteem.

Kids who bounce back assume the problem is a misunderstanding that they can straighten out, that they need to apologize, or that the other child must just be in a bad mood.

Limited responses

If you watch children play together for a while, you'll notice that some have a pretty limited and ineffective repertoire of responses to the inevitable spats that crop up. Over and over again they resort to hitting, grabbing, or crying, even though these actions don't accomplish what they want. Others, no matter what their age, are more successful in handling mean kids, because they try different strategies and responses until they find one that does work well (see pages 54-65).

The environment contributes

In an atmosphere where teachers and parents constantly compare and categorize children by their talents, grades, looks, and family background, teasing, cliques, and put-downs flourish, and kids become more sensitive to taunts that might not hurt them under other circumstances. At one affluent private school in New York City, where this kind of comparison goes on regularly, putting down others for not having things like an expensive haircut, a new backpack, or pants or shirts that sport a designer label starts as early as second grade.

Exclusive groups and cliques begin at an earlier age in large schools than in small ones, but being "out" in a very tiny school may hurt more. Why? The number of kids isn't large enough to support more than one "in" group, so kids who are "out" end up with no group at all. ❏

Are Some Kinds Of Kids Picked On More Often?

During their years in elementary and middle school children spend most of their time with other kids, both schoolmates and siblings, learning how to get along. In this process, few relationships progress completely smoothly. But several kinds of kids do seem to be picked on more than others.

Kids who are different

Larry has a learning problem, which no one discovered until second grade. Because he has so much difficulty with reading, he spends an hour each day in the resource room with a learning specialist. Last year, whenever he stumbled over words while reading aloud, several kids in the

class started calling him "dummy" and "retard." This year they do it even more.

Differences of any kind make many kids uncomfortable. Most of us have observed children trying to distance themselves from anyone who doesn't fit into the class and school norms as though their problems were contagious. Unless a school takes a strong stance against it, kids often rely on teasing and name-calling to make clear they're not "like Larry."

Children with speech and hearing difficulties or poor coordination, who are short for their age or overweight, who speak with an accent, are from a different ethnic group, or have another skin color may be singled out. Smart kids are often picked on, too, especially in middle school.

Being the new kid at school is another way of being different (see pages 84-85).

If your child fits into one of these categories, you can help best by coaching him in how to respond and work on ways he can feel good about himself.

Kids who just don't "fit in"

Throughout elementary school, no matter how hard Lindsay has tried to be part of things, kids have called her a "weirdo." They don't actually pick on her anymore; they just ignore her.

Some children, like Lindsay, don't seem to "fit in" right from the beginning of school. It isn't because they don't want to.

They just can't seem to hit on the right way of doing things to belong. Bewildered and confused about other kids' reactions to them, they don't understand why no one likes them. Other kids may find it hard to explain why they avoid these kids, too. "Lindsay's just weird, Mom," one girl said in exasperation. "She acts strange. Like she's always pushing up against you."

Lindsay had a knack for laughing too loud at nothing, interpreted a sad expression as an angry one, and didn't seem to realize she was leaning right into someone's face. In addition, she wore skirts instead of the leggings and long shirts favored by most of the girls in her class. She was out of sync with her classmates. Her behavior made them feel uneasy, so they avoided her.

Like Lindsay, many kids who don't "fit in" don't understand the kinds of nonverbal communication that so many of us take for granted. And that's important because, as researchers have found, kids— in fact, all of us—pay more attention to nonverbal language than to what people actually say.

How your children dress, how loud they laugh and when, the expressions on their faces, the kinds of gestures they use, how close they stand to someone in a lunch line, whether their hair is combed or not—all these make up a message that other people "read" and react to. Most of us don't give much thought to these

ASK THE EXPERTS

Drs. Marshall P. Duke and Stephen Nowicki, Jr. , child psychologists at Emory University in Atlanta, found that as many as 1 in 10 children have problems with nonverbal communication.

How can you tell?
- **Teachers describe these children as tactless or socially immature.**
- **Other children tend to call them "dumb," though they are of average or above average intelligence.**
- **These children don't always understand rules or see a connection between their behavior and its consequences.**

Nowicki and Duke suggest parents try the following to help their kids learn to read nonverbal cues better:
- **Watch TV together. Turn the sound off, then take turns guessing what's going on and how the actors feel.**
- **Watch other kids on the playground and in the mall with your child. Ask him to guess how they are feeling.**

others give, and don't know how to give off the right messages themselves.

Fortunately you can help children learn these nonverbal skills. But they also need to spend time with other children. If a child is around adults most of the time, he or she may have a great deal of trouble picking up on the cues of peers.

Kids who are anxious

Nate is quiet and cautious, sensitive, small, and not very strong for his age, which is eleven. He is usually worried about something and whines and complains a lot. When his older brothers call him "worry wart" and tease him, he gets upset but doesn't do much to defend himself. Nate has some of the characteristics of kids who are the frequent target of serious bullying.

Difficult as it is for parents to accept, children who are chronically bullied sometimes seem to fit a particular personality profile and behave in ways that attract bullies. Like Nate, they are more anxious, nervous, and insecure than other kids, lack social skills, are physically weak, and cry and give in when others pick on them. The way they act around others communicates vulnerability and fear.

Parents can help children like Nate learn to respond better to a bully (see pages 54-65), but they also need to encourage them to be more confident and independent and to find a few friends. ❏

things. We react instinctively to them without analyzing exactly what it is we're reacting to. Kids who don't fit in don't know how to read the nonverbal messages

The immediate consequences of the little daily meannesses in our children's lives are all too apparent to parents. Sometimes it's temporary outrage and fury, the way Tony felt when his younger brother deliberately scribbled on a favorite drawing. Sometimes it's a deluge of tears and sadness, as Katrina experienced when her best friend abandoned her for someone more popular.

Hurt, disappointment, sadness, anger, humiliation, helplessness, and embarrassment are not easy feelings for children—or adults—to live through, even for a short time. But for the most part, children learn from them and discover that when someone is mean, it's not the end of the world.

But how much does the mean behavior of others over time affect our kids' views of themselves? What happens to the ones who are rejected over and over or are teased or bullied for three months or even a year or more?

What Happens To Kids Who Are Frequently Left Out & Teased?

Memories of meanness last

Just think back to your own childhood. You may be surprised at how much mean incidents still sting. For years when I made a speech in front of an audience, a memory from seventh grade would come flooding into my mind. As I walked out onto the stage to recite the Gettysburg Address, which I had spent a couple of weeks memorizing, a boy (never mind who) tripped me, and I fell flat on my face. The whole school laughed, and I felt totally embarrassed and humiliated.

In the years between five and thirteen, other kids, both siblings and classmates, comprise our kids' world for most of their waking hours. How our kids fit in and how others treat them have a powerful impact on how they see themselves. Some manage to weave their way through those relationships skillfully, hanging on to their self-esteem. Others decide "I must be a nerd" or "No one likes me." Seventh and eighth graders have no trouble dredging up details of the time David punched them in first grade and their nose bled, the way Ellen called them "fat blob" in third, and how their three oldest friends went on a beach picnic without them in fifth.

Long-term consequences

Being picked on every day or left out regularly or teased about being flat-chested for a few months can hamper learning and leave deep scars. If your child is worrying about whether a bully is going to humiliate him after school or someone in his math class is going to make fun of him when he makes a mistake, he won't be able to concentrate much on his schoolwork. If your child never has anyone to sit with at lunch, she may not want to go to school and develop all sorts of symptoms so she can stay home.

Many children who are bullied feel worthless and helpless to protect themselves. They are far more likely than other students to bring a weapon to school to defend themselves. Those who are left out feel lonely, anxious, depressed, and insecure, and they don't have the opportunity to practice the kinds of social and emotional skills they'll need later in life. Both tend to look upon themselves as failures and often don't measure up to their academic potential in school.

When you think about it, what adult could work well at an office where one of his co-workers insulted him every day or no one wanted to eat lunch with him?

Experts believe that even one year as a victim or outcast can damage a child's future at school. Reputations cling. Vulnerable children who are continually shut out are likely to be further rejected as they go from grade to grade. Kids who've been bullied sometimes carry their feelings of low self-esteem into adulthood. ❑

WHAT TO DO

The Best Advice

How To Find Out What's Going On

My son drooped around the house with a tight look on his face for several days before I elicited, over milk and chocolate chip cookies, the story about the mean kid on the school bus. It took me a while to grasp just what this boy had done and how upset my son was. That's not unusual—we all know how hard it is to get an accurate and complete story of the actions among children, no matter what their ages. My immediate concern—as it is for most parents—was to figure out whether my son was hurt and how serious the problem was. That's not always easy.

Some kids are complainers

Consider the difficulty of finding out the truth behind these accusations during a family Thanksgiving gathering: "Eliza never stops calling me 'monkey face.'" "Jimmy shut Tony in the bathroom and wouldn't let him out. He laughed when Tony cried!" "Becky keeps kicking me under the table." "Ned is always such a bully—I feel like killing him." Some turned out to be much bigger problems than others. Like many kids, these cousins dramatize and see others' mean behavior in the apocalyptic terms of "always" and "never." They sometimes misinterpret other children's actions and find it hard to recognize when their

own are provocative. The most sensitive ones react strongly when they are teased, even if it's only once, and become so emotional it's hard to tell who did what to whom and when.

Some kids don't tell

But many kids, like my son, don't talk without considerable encouragement. With them you have to watch for kid clues that something is wrong. Why?

Younger children sometimes don't have enough social experience to understand someone else's behavior. If a situation is new or confusing, they may not know why they are upset or have the vocabulary to explain. When shy, five-year-old Lauren started kindergarten, for example, another girl, who said she was Lauren's friend, threatened to punch Lauren if she didn't sit next to her at snack time and warned, "A big blue goose will bite your eyes out if you play house with Tina instead of me." Her mother finally realized there was a problem when Lauren tearfully insisted she wanted to go to a different school.

Other kids, particularly those over nine, keep their hurt, anger, or fear to themselves because they are ashamed and embarrassed. They think they should be able to handle the problem themselves. That's how ten-year-old Ryan felt when his two best friends started teasing him about his chubbiness. But he did tell his parents,

"I'm just a loser; no one likes me anymore"—a clear sign that he was troubled.

Children who are seriously bullied rarely confide their problem to parents, even when they are regularly coming home with bruises, dirty clothes, and missing books and lunch money. Instead, they typically offer excuses when their parents inquire about these signs of abuse.

The most common reasons are being ashamed and that preteen code of silence: "Don't tell an adult." Being known as a tattletale is a disgrace, worse than being bullied. And they all fear that if their parents try to intervene, the bullying—whether it's teasing or physical beatings—will get worse. The truth is, if adults intervene in an ineffective way, it probably will.

Listen with empathy

In our house, as in many others, a hug, a gentle inquiry about why my son looks sad, and a time when we can be alone without interruptions create the best setting for getting the whole story.

I've found that the most important thing is to listen first and try to understand what happened from your child's point of view. Kids are always more likely to spill out the details and their own feelings if we take their concerns seriously, no matter how trivial they may seem to us. Saying that we can imagine how much someone's meanness must hurt and how angry, hurt, or embarrassed they must feel lets kids know we understand and can be counted on for help.

It's easy for parents to think, if their child is being called "chubby" or "a walking dictionary," for example, or didn't have anyone to sit with at lunch, that the teasing or rejection doesn't sound so terrible. But from your child's point of view it may be devastating. Maybe he should be able to take it in stride. But if it has been going on for a long time or your child is young or very sensitive, he may not be able to fix things without your help. If your child seems to be complaining a lot about being teased or picked on or left out, you need to figure out why.

On the other hand, it's hard not to over-react if someone is beating up or threatening your child! Staying calm, letting your child know that you are angry about what's going on, and telling him that this kind of behavior is completely wrong are essential.

In getting the story, be patient—it's hard for kids to talk about something that upsets them—and accept what your kids tell you as fact. Maybe the problem isn't as serious as they think it is, but that's how serious it *feels* to them.

Whatever mean behavior your children are experiencing, make sure you reassure them that you will help them figure out how to stop it.

Share an experience

Our children also need to hear that it's normal to be upset about being teased, bullied, or left out and that feeling that way doesn't mean they are wimps. Hearing about the time the most obnoxious boy in my class deliberately dribbled soda down the back of my brand-new jacket on a school bus trip, how upset I was, and that I didn't know what to do made my son much more comfortable in telling me *his*

> ## ▶ PARENT TIPS
>
> *"I try to get my son to understand there's more than one way to explain the other child's behavior,"* says Mary, a New York City mother. She always asks:
>
> ▶ What was the other person trying to do?
> ▶ Did he really intend to be mean?
> ▶ How could you find out? What did he say and do?
> ▶ Is that always a mean thing?

story. When I told him my mom had helped me figure out what to do, he was more willing to believe that I could help him. After all, I'd had experience!

Ask for specifics

Only after listening compassionately and being supportive should you ask about the specific details: Who is being mean? What does he or she do? How did you feel about it—angry, hurt, scared? What did you do about it—cry, tease back, say how you felt? Did that work? Do any teachers know? If so, what did they do or say?

Before you can help children figure out what to do, you need a reality check. Has your child been teased just once and found it hard to handle, or has teasing become a daily event? Does it sound as though your child might be misinterpreting a situation or might even be provoking it? Is your child being picked on during an unsupervised recess or bothered by a neighborhood bully on the way to school? Keep in mind that you may have to ask a teacher or another parent for her perspective on a younger child's story.

If your child is a preteen or the problem is serious, write everything down, including dates, times, and what happened. If he's been beaten up, take a photo.

For physical bullying, make an official complaint to the school (see pages 66-69), but also help your child select and practice the tactics discussed on pages 54-65. ❏

ASK THE EXPERTS

Research psychologist Dr. Dorothea Ross, author of *Childhood Bullying and Teasing*, **points out several mistakes parents make when it comes to teasing:**

● **They minimize how serious it is. Some parents make jokes—suggesting flippantly that their kids think of it as "just a blip on the computer screen of life"—and don't offer suggestions for what to do, probably because they don't know. But the combination of no sympathy, no advice, and teasing makes kids feel terribly alone.**
● **They let kids down by telling them that everyone gets teased, it's their problem, and to stand up for them-selves. They don't recognize that being teased over time is highly stressful and that kids sometimes need help learn-ing to stand up for themselves.**
● **They call the teaser and sometimes "reward" him by inviting him over to discuss the problem and even "nego-tiate" with him to stop by offering special privileges.**
● **They call the teaser's parents to complain. Unless these parents are very sympathetic people, this approach usually results in the child being thought of as a tattletale and a wimp, and he is teased even more.**

Start With Problem Solving

Except in instances of serious bullying, it's best to think of yourself as a problem-solving coach whose job is to work with your children so they can handle the problem themselves. First, of course, you have to understand their view of what the problem is and how they feel about it.

Tyler, a fifth grader, was miserable at recess. Mike, a much bigger kid, often called him a "sissy" in front of other kids on the playground. Tyler was embarrassed and got so angry that he usually tried to punch Mike, even though his efforts at retaliation were weak and ineffectual. Mike knew he was stronger; he just laughed

and then hit Tyler back and knocked him down. "I have to hit Mike," Tyler told his dad. "Otherwise everyone will think I really am a sissy!"

Rachel, a third grader, felt miserable during recess, too. Gina, Molly, and Vicky, the bossiest girls in her grade, put themselves in charge of organizing the fantasy games many of the girls liked to play. Rachel wanted to join in, but the three always assigned her the most unwanted roles, like the "slimy snail," the "captured slave," or the "baby." Some days Rachel cried and said she

didn't want the assigned role, but gave in anyway. On other days she got angry, refused to play, and sat alone, watching. She told her mom, "Gina, Molly, and Vicky are mean. I hate recess. I never have any fun."

Rachel wanted to play at recess but couldn't figure out any other options—how to negotiate for a different role, for example, or how to find some other interesting activity for herself. Tyler wanted Mike to stop bothering him but believed the only solution was hitting Mike. Many kids, like Rachel and Tyler, react in the same way over and over again—being upset and crying, getting angry and hitting back (often ineffectually), or giving in and backing off. Since these reactions are just what most mean kids are counting on, they don't stop their behavior.

The value of problem solving

One thing that distinguishes children who handle "mean kid" problems well is their resourcefulness in negotiating and problem solving: they see several ways of responding to a difficult situation and keep trying strategies until they find one that works.

Problem solving is a thinking process that doesn't come naturally to most children, but it's one we need to help them learn. Developing and using step-by-step strategies to insure positive results in many areas of their lives—school, making friends, getting along with parents, in addition to dealing

with mean kids—is highly important for all children between the ages of five and thirteen. Some are better than others at planning for success. Many, for example, carefully observe the way other children manage to resolve situations, study for a test, make a friend, or get along with a teacher, and copy those strategies. Others have had some experience that helped them realize what else they could do. Most, however, still require coaching from parents.

If you first listen thoughtfully, ask questions to get the whole story, and reassure children that you're on their side, though, they're much more likely to be able to think of solutions.

Brainstorm solutions

Once you get the problem clarified, ask your children to come up with other ways they could respond the next time the situation arises. Sometimes it helps to actually list children's suggestions on a piece of paper. One part of problem solving is postponing judgment until you have several solutions to consider, so don't worry if some are silly, inappropriate, or even vindictive. If children have a tough time coming up with ideas, as Rachel did, read a few books or watch a video about characters who have similar problems (see pages 92-96). Discuss what they did. Could their solutions work for your child, too?

ASK THE EXPERTS

According to Dr. Myrna B. Shure, a developmental psychologist at Allegheny University and author of *Raising a Thinking Child* (Pocket Books, 1996):

• You want to get kids thinking, instead of reacting automatically. Then they can begin to see being teased or bullied or left out as a problem to be solved, not as something inevitable they can't do anything about.

• If children learn to define a problem, then take charge in devising solutions, they come to see themselves as having the power to change the situation.

• Children are less likely to carry out ideas when we do the thinking and suggesting for them. They're more likely to follow through on ideas they come up with themselves.

• Reinforce the process of problem solving instead of focusing on a single solution. Then if one doesn't work, children have a way to think of another.

• Remember that emotions can block out attempts to think at any given moment.

Tyler's dad suggested he look for other options by being a detective at school and keeping track of his observations. Does Mike call any other kids "sissy"? What do other kids do when they are called names or shoved? Does Mike always hang out in the same part of the playground? He gave Tyler a small notebook to keep track of exactly what Mike did and said, so they could talk about what else might have worked. In the process Tyler began to look at Mike in a more objective way—instead of just reacting.

One of the most common solutions kids try on their own is simply avoiding the mean kid, but often it doesn't work.

Think through the consequences

The next step is to think through the consequences of each solution on the list and pick the one to try. Rachel's solutions, for example, included getting mad at Molly, Gina, and Vicky and not speaking to them anymore; negotiating with them to play the unwanted roles twice a week if Rachel could have other roles the other three days; playing jacks during recess with two girls who weren't interested in fantasy games; and telling the three girls she didn't think they were playing fair.

Her mom asked about each one: "If you do that, what might the girls do?" "How will you feel?" "What might stop that from working?" Rachel decided that she really didn't want to play jacks during recess—her first choice was playing the fantasy game. Though she was mad at the three girls, she knew that stomping off and not talking to them wouldn't get her new roles in the game. If I tell them they are unfair, she thought, they'll just say, "So?" or something mean. Her best bet of getting different roles, she decided, was negotiating.

Pages 50-65 offer a variety of solutions children have used when kids have been mean to them.

Make a plan and try it

Once kids choose what to do, they need to break it down into smaller steps. With her mom's help, Rachel planned to talk to the girls before recess.

She worked out what to say, what to offer and what do if they said no, and practiced in advance (see pages 60-61). The next morning, as she left for school, her mom said warmly, "Let me know whether your negotiation solution works."

This time, it did, but as adults know, even a good solution won't always work when other people are involved. Then we have to help our children evaluate why it didn't and try another.

Be realistic

Consider your child's age, abilities, personality, and the seriousness of the problem when trying to help him or her create a plan. A skinny seventh grader being teased because he just grew six inches can probably manage to stop the teasing on his own with some coaching. Researchers have found that even preschoolers can learn to use problem solving for simple everyday conflicts. But a frightened six-year-old who is threatened by a fourth-grade bully on the school bus requires help from adults. ❑

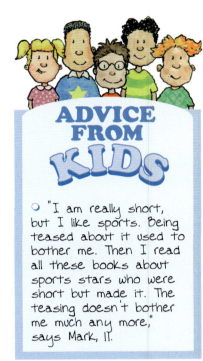

ADVICE FROM KIDS

○ "I am really short, but I like sports. Being teased about it used to bother me. Then I read all these books about sports stars who were short but made it. The teasing doesn't bother me much any more," says Mark, 11.

When Your Child Feels Left Out

◆ One-half of all boys rejected by their peers are described by them as aggressive.

◆ Children who suffer from depression are likely to be either rejected or neglected by others.

◆ How popular a child is in 3rd grade better predicts problems with mental health at age 18 than psychological tests do.

◆ Rejected kids are half as likely to have a best friend during grade school.

◆ Young children sometimes play out their fears of being outsiders by rejecting others.

"No one likes me." "Joelle wouldn't let me play at recess." "Ruth and Ellen totally dumped me after school." "Danny didn't pick me for his team." "Jane is having a major party and didn't invite me!" When children moan these complaints, parents feel terrible. If our children spend most of their time alone and the phone hardly ever rings for them, we worry even if they don't complain about being lonely or show that they feel upset.

Some rejection seems to be a natural part of negotiating friendships and requires sympathy and minimal coaching on your part. But when it is a pattern that lasts over a few weeks or several months or more, the first thing to do is figure out how your child feels about being rejected and why it may be happening.

Are your child's perceptions accurate?

Many children are quick to interpret every slight as an intentional rejection. When seven-year-old Lisa tells Melissa she'll play catch at recess but instead runs off with Samantha, Melissa is angry, convinced Lisa is shutting her out deliberately. She tells her mom, "Lisa doesn't like me anymore."

But maybe Lisa just forgot. Some of our children have a hard time learning that friends don't always live up to our expectations, but may still remain friends. By seven to nine years of age, kids should be developing a more complex view of friend-

ship as something that doesn't have to end if they run into a conflict.

But saying, "Don't be silly, of course she still likes you," probably won't make your rejected child feel better. Instead, restate the problem and try to get your child to think through what happened and what her other options were, as Melissa's mom did. Ask questions such as: Why do you think she left you out? What else could you have done? Could you have played with someone else? We can also help our children find alternate ways of thinking about being excluded. Maybe Lisa isn't looking for a friend right now, but someone else probably is.

Feeling shy

Shy, timid children sometimes end up as social outcasts. Their anxiety in approaching others is a matter of temperament, but studies have shown that parents can help them to be more outgoing. How? Coach them in being more assertive (see pages 56-57) and in social skills (see pages 81-83) and praise them for any step they take, such as inviting a classmate over once a week. Acknowledge their fears, but treat shyness as a behavior they can change.

Nurture one friendship

Children need friends, but they don't have to have ten. Having one friend or several or a different friend each week are all

experts recommend helping them establish a friendship with one other child. Researchers have found that a child of any age is most likely to be accepted by either a single child or a group of at least four.

For younger children, ask the teacher to be a matchmaker and suggest an appropriate child for you to invite over for a play-date. Short visits have a greater chance of success than long ones. If you keep an eye on what is going on, you can help them over rough moments. Don't forget to praise your child for his efforts. When you plan special family events, such as going to the zoo, encourage your child to bring the friend along.

Older elementary kids are likely to meet a friend with similar interests in scout troups, clubs, or after-school programs where excluding is more difficult because of adult supervision. Going this route is especially important for children who are rejected because they are very different from most of their classmates—an artistic boy in a class full of jocks, for example.

"normal" for children between the ages of five and thirteen, and one friend is all it takes for a child to feel insulated against rejection. With shy kids or kids who are caught in a pattern of being left out,

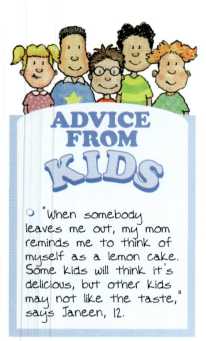

ADVICE FROM KIDS

o "When somebody leaves me out, my mom reminds me to think of myself as a lemon cake. Some kids will think it's delicious, but other kids may not like the taste," says Janeen, 12.

Practice social skills

Seeing how her son acted with the other boys on the school hike, Margaret began to understand why other children rarely invited him over. Charlie insisted on being the first to jump over the brook, refused to share his binoculars, and protested when everyone else wanted to stop for a break. She realized that Charlie, like many kids who are left out, needed more practice with social skills (see pages 81-83). After they read a few books about friends, she helped Charlie set up positive steps to take so kids would like him better. Bragging, showing off, being a poor loser, and not knowing how to make others feel good are typical behaviors of unpopular children.

Sometimes children who have trouble "fitting in" are doing other things to turn kids off. They may need help learning how to interpret others' nonverbal messages and send appropriate ones (see pages 37-38).

When friends boss and manipulate

Watching our children submit to a friend's domination for fear of being rejected is particularly painful for many parents. The bossy child may always insist on being the star or on deciding when and what the two will play, and regularly threaten not to talk to your child or be her friend if she doesn't comply. Most parents wonder: Doesn't my child see what's going on? Should I refuse to let her play with this friend? Children

ASK THE EXPERTS

Dr. Thomas J. Berndt, a professor of psychology at Purdue University and an expert on children's friendships, suggests that if your middle-school child is being rejected from a group:

• Your child may be aiming at a large, well-established group whose members don't want anyone else. She needs to set her sights at a more appropriate group.
• Your child may have refused invitations too often. She needs to extend a few invitations and for a while accept all those she receives.
• Your child may be too competitive and unwilling to compromise.
• Arrange events such as a beach trip for your child and her friends. If you accompany them, you'll be able to observe how she relates to others.

in this predicament often confess that the friendship doesn't "feel right" but are worried about having no friends at all if they end it. Instead of forbidding it, help a child learn to stand up for herself (see pages 56-57) and widen her circle of friends.

Losing a friend

When close friendships break apart, the breakup is not usually mutual, and one child ends up feeling rejected. Most parents underestimate what a crisis losing a friend is to their children, assuring them, "Don't worry, you'll find another friend."

It's better to let your child know you understand how hard losing a friend is and talk about why it happened. To younger children, the fact that a friend no longer wants to play with them can be devastating, because they don't understand why. The reason is rarely a single fight or incident. Instead, a rift happens gradually, often because one child finds she now has more in common with another.

Researchers have found that kids who feel rejection most keenly are those who blame themselves—or others' meanness—instead of recognizing that a friend has, for example, become interested in girls, while they're still hanging out in a treehouse.

Build self-confidence

Much of children's self-esteem in elementary and middle school depends on their relationships with other kids and feeling accepted. When someone tells them they can't play or be part of a group, their self-image plummets. But children who feel confident about themselves more easily weather the inevitable hurt feelings when they're left out of an activity and more readily solve these kinds of problems themselves. If one particular child doesn't want to be their friend, they say to themselves: "If she doesn't want to be my friend, I won't die. I'll just try somebody else."

One of the best ways to build self-confidence, especially for children who are outsiders at school, is to help them find a sport or other activity in which to shine. ❑

▶ PARENT TIPS

Joan G., mother of a 6th and an 8th grader, suggests:

▶ Don't pile on sympathy for every tiny hurt or kids will assume they've been terribly wronged.

▶ Don't get overly involved if your child is shut out of a clique. For example, don't call another child's mother and ask her to make sure your child is invited to a party.

▶ Find out how upset your child really is before you assume he or she must feel terrible.

▶ Don't project your own social expectations on your children! Maybe they'll never be as popular as you wish they were—or you wanted to be as a child.

Kid Tactics 1: Stay Calm & Ignore It

At the end of lunch three eighth-grade boys surrounded Kevin, a sixth grader, just outside the cafeteria door and chanted, "Fat butt, fat butt," as he headed to his locker. Kevin dropped his books, put his hands over his ears, and looked at the floor so they couldn't see him struggling not to cry, but his distress was so apparent that the boys all laughed at him.

When he went home terribly upset, his mom and dad told him his reaction was just what the boys wanted. They were right. Many kids who are picked on, like Kevin, reward a mean kid with tears, anger, or evident fear. That emotional payoff is what a bully is looking for to feel superior and be the one in control.

Experts have found that a lot of mean behavior, such as teasing, ridiculing, and bullying, follows a progression of steps—even in preschool. A teaser tries an exploratory insult or two, and if your child whines, cries, looks embarrassed or afraid, or gets mad and strikes out, the teasing accelerates. As many of us have observed at home, the more emotionally a child reacts, the more the teaser is liable to tease, whether he is a classmate or a sibling.

Sometimes this pattern gets set as early as preschool, and a child's reputation as a crybaby carries over from one year to the next. With older kids, a pattern of teasing can escalate fairly quickly into more serious bullying attacks.

Ways kids can stay calm

Kids with calm and peaceable temperaments often slough off hurtful and sarcastic remarks, rejection, and other taunts the first time another child tries them because they have better control over their emotions. Staying calm instead of crying is a tall order for others, especially those who are younger, shy and sensitive, or excitable and hot-tempered.

The old methods of counting to ten or taking three deep breaths are two ways for children of all ages to calm themselves down. My preferred method at age seven, when the taunting power of the eleven-year-old boy who lived next door reached its height, was counting backwards from twenty very, very slowly, which took more concentration.

Talking silently to yourself is another method to teach kids. Repeating "I'm a good person, and I'm not going to let this kid get to me," or "Cool down—I'm strong enough to handle this," or "I'm too smart to give this kid what he wants" gives children positive thoughts to focus on and keeps them feeling good about themselves. Even children in kindergarten and first grade can learn to tell themselves, "Calm down," or "Stop and think."

Recalling a happy experience or pleasant scene is also soothing and calming. Young children might think about snuggling with a favorite stuffed animal in a big comfy chair or blowing out the candles at their last birthday party; older kids might focus on lying on the beach looking at the waves or relaxing on the grass after playing a game of baseball.

Ignoring is hard

Just about every parent I know has told his or her children at least once: "Just ignore that mean kid. Say to yourself, 'Sticks and stones will break my bones, but names will never hurt me.'" As my son once pointed out to me, this isn't true. Names *do* hurt, sometimes a lot. And ignoring someone who is being mean and horrible to you is much harder than it sounds.

Staying calm and not reacting is the first step. Remaining silent is another part of an effective ignoring strategy. Since that's so difficult for children of all ages, psychologist Dr. Dorothea Ross suggests they also show their total disinterest in the child who is taunting them by yawning, appearing very interested in or laughing at something else that's going on nearby, or walking away briskly without even looking in his or her direction.

The hard part of the ignoring tactic is that when children first use it, the mean behavior usually gets meaner. The boys picking on Kevin tried even harder to make him upset, calling "chicken" loudly when he looked at them silently, then walked away down the hall. Every day he told himself, "I can outlast them. I know what's going on and what they're trying to do to me." It took two unpleasant weeks before they finally stopped.

How to make ignoring work

Because this tactic often takes as much as several weeks to work and children have to be able to withstand the increase in meanness without crumpling in the meantime, they need a lot of practice (see pages 60-61), praise, and support from their family. Every evening when Kevin reported how the band of eighth graders had stepped up its attacks but he hadn't reacted, his dad gave him a "high five," complimented him on his control, and marked off another successful day on the calendar.

Not all children, especially younger ones, can manage this tactic right away. The more you encourage them to stay calm in situations when they become frustrated, angry, or annoyed at home, the more control they'll gain and the more they'll be able to use that control elsewhere. But assess your children's ages and abilities as well as the problem before suggesting they use it in a tough situation.

Staying calm and ignoring are strategies that work for teasing, insults, and name-calling, and are key tactics for many kinds of rejection, but if your child is punched or kicked by a bully, you need to intervene on his or her behalf (see pages 64-69). ❑

ADVICE FROM KIDS

○ "When kids tease, I imagine I'm a big tree. I imagine their words are the wind blowing through the branches, but they can't hurt the tree," says Melissa, 7.

○ "A boy in my class kept calling me a 'dork.' My dad told me to think about the time I made a goal in soccer and everybody cheered when I did," says Matt, 10.

○ "Some girls were cutting me out and making mean remarks about my clothes. I told myself, 'they'll get tired of this if you don't react. You can handle it. You have other friends,'" explains Tessa, 13.

Kid Tactics 2: Be Assertive

Most of us are so busy teaching our children not to be aggressive that we forget to teach them to be assertive—to stand up for themselves without fighting. This is another skill that our kids need in order to combat others' meanness effectively.

Every time eight-year-old Meghan practiced the songs for her solo in the class concert, her older brother made withering remarks like, "Your voice is pathetic! No one will be able to hear it. A frog can croak better than that."

Meghan felt terrible and complained to her dad, who told her, "When your brother is mean to you, you have to call him on it, Meghan. You can tell Craig, 'I feel hurt and sad when people make fun of my singing. I don't like it. Stop doing it.'"

We don't want our children to let others, either their siblings or friends, trample on their feelings, take things from them, or hit them. Being assertive is a way of saying, "I have a right to be respected." When others act mean, assertive kids state what they don't like in a confident, straightforward manner, describe how these actions make them feel, and are clear about the fact that they want them to end.

Identify how your kids feel

Like Meghan, many kids have trouble sorting out and talking about their emotions, whether they're angry and hurt by a friend gossiping about them or embarrassed because they're being teased about what they wear. Meghan didn't know what to say to her brother, nor did she know how to say it so it would have an impact on him. Some kids are afraid to tell others face-to-face how they feel and what they want, even when they get into a spat with a good friend. Instead they whine, run away, or complain bitterly to their parents, none of which help.

Middle-school issues

In middle school, put-down banter is one way kids communicate, part of the tough facade they put on to cover up their new feelings of vulnerability and self-consciousness. Saying "You idiot" to classmates who make mistakes in math or riding kids who miss a shot in a basketball game or strike out in baseball are par for the course. But many students don't know when and how to let others know that they've crossed a line and the joke is no longer funny.

This is particularly true with regard to the sexual teasing that's typical of kids in middle school. Girls, for example, may be highly embarrassed by a boy's crude remarks about the size of their breasts or upset by a boy grabbing their buttocks in the hall, yet endure in silence. We need to tell them that they're in charge of setting the boundaries for their own bodies, and that they can tell others to keep their hands off.

Plan what to say

Anticipation and practice are essential. Once your child decides how she feels, help her compose and memorize several short statements she could say, such as, "I don't like that you're spreading rumors about me and trying to get people not to like me. It's unfair. I want you to stop it." After she says it, she should break off eye contact with the other person and walk away quickly.

Even shy children or those as young as five or six years of age can act more assertive if they have thought about what they want to say in advance. They're more likely to remember and use statements they've dreamed up themselves.

Coach how to say it

Body language and tone of voice count, whether children are kindergartners or middle schoolers. As all parents know from talking to their own kids, you have to look and sound as though you mean what you say. No matter what words he uses, your son won't appear confident if he hunches over, has a worried expression on his face, mumbles in a soft voice, and fidgets.

Coach your kids to look assertive, too, by showing them how to appear relaxed and in charge:

- *Look people in the eye.*
- *Stand up straight, with feet slightly apart.*
- *Keep your hands in your pockets.*
- *Move closer to the person rather than backing off as you talk.*
- *Speak loudly enough and use a firm and determined voice.*

To help kids come up with some of their own ideas, ask questions like: How could you say that in a way that would make the bully really listen to you?

Taking karate and judo classes often helps children who are being bullied develop a more confident stance.

Pick the right situation

It's easier for kids to be assertive and impress a mean kid if they catch him alone. Bullies are more likely to back down if they are not performing for others and a group isn't around to egg them on. But a girl who is confronting a boy about his sexual remarks will have more success if she asks other girls to be with her.

Being assertive is a good basic strategy for kids of all ages to start with, especially for gossip, teasing, mild threats, mean tricks, sexual teasing, or rejection by a close friend, or rude or unfair treatment by a friend. But when mean behavior involves physical violence, being assertive can sometimes make the situation worse. And accept that some kids, especially if they are young or shy, may be too frightened to be assertive without a teacher or parent coaching them and actually being present when they try it in an encounter. ❑

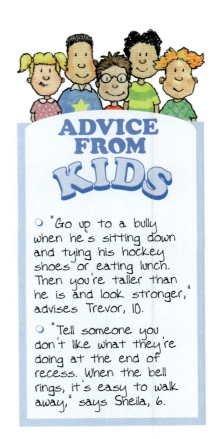

ADVICE FROM KIDS

- "Go up to a bully when he's sitting down and tying his hockey shoes or eating lunch. Then you're taller than he is and look stronger," advises Trevor, 10.

- "Tell someone you don't like what they're doing at the end of recess. When the bell rings, it's easy to walk away," says Sheila, 6.

Kid Tactics 3: Use Comebacks

Ignoring, staying calm, and being assertive are not always enough with mean kids, especially in middle school. Sometimes kids need—and want—a quick retort to turn the tables. That's when comebacks are useful—as they were for Ben, an eighth grader in a Chicago suburb who dreaded gym class because a taller boy kept harassing him. At the end of gym, Ben would find his clothes in a heap on the floor just outside his locker. But what he hated most was the way the boy waited until Ben turned his back, then quickly moved in close, grabbed the top of Ben's underwear, and pulled it up as hard as he could until it ripped. In his school this was known as "doing an undy grundy." Ben told his mom, "It's so humiliating. All the other kids laugh."

Together with his parents Ben dreamed up a comeback that worked. The next time the boy circled behind Ben, ready to grab his underwear, Ben said in a very loud, very disgusted voice, "Get your filthy hands off me, you creep."

The result: everyone in the locker room turned to look at the harasser and began taunting him with remarks like "Hey, can't keep your hands to yourself? Whoo-hoo!" A few days of this response was all it took to stop the bullying.

Doing something unexpected the way Ben did is one type of comeback that frequently works. Here are three more that

many experts—and several kids—recommend: agreeing, breaking the pattern, and counterattacking. All take much practice, because they depend on children staying calm and having confidence.

They're for use in situations, again, where physical bullying, serious threats, and extorting money or possessions are not the issue.

Agree or give permission

If kids are being teased or harassed for something that's true—they really are chubby or have freckles or wear glasses or are short—simply agreeing takes a teaser off guard and takes away much of his power and reason for teasing. That's what Al, a very short twelve-year-old, did whenever boys in his class teased him about his height. He would look very interested and say in a tolerant, matter-of-fact way, "Yes, I'm short. I'm amazed you noticed! What else have you noticed about short people? Anything interesting?" No matter what anyone said, he simply kept agreeing he was short in an unemotional way, even offering his exact height, until the other kids got tired of taunting.

Teasers also get annoyed when kids simply tell them to go on teasing. Suzanne would smile and say in a condescending way, "If you want to say that, go right ahead," or pronounce in a grand, queenly manner, "I grant you the right to say that," when a classmate made fun of her frizzy hair. No matter what the classmate said, Suzanne repeated some variation of those words until the teasing eventually stopped.

Like ignoring, these strategies require a fair amount of practice for kids to be able to employ them effectively, and it may take two weeks or even more before they end the teasing.

Break the pattern

When kids can anticipate what a bully or mean kid is going to do and when, they can sometimes make a change in their own routine that breaks the pattern and prevents the behavior from happening. This is a kind of silent comeback. Two six-year-old girls decided to wear long pants to school for a while after a group of boys chased them and pulled up their skirts. James persuaded his big brother to walk with him to school every day after a bully waylaid him and took his new hat.

Use counterattacks

It's best for kids to use the following counterattacks in front of others because the point is either to embarrass the person who's teasing or harassing or to convey to everyone that the teaser is of absolutely no importance in the grand scheme of things, an approach my mother favored. One of her favorite responses when I complained about someone's meanness was, "Just consider the source, dear." Her main advice

was to turn the tease back at the person who was teasing. It worked when I was ten and still does, based on the experiences of several kids I know who have tried it.

Basically you listen, then smile, fold your arms, and say in a fake-nice, fake-sympathetic way, "I guess it takes one to know one," or "You think I have freckles—have you looked at your nose?" or "Hmm. Think my shirt is funny? What about the one you have on?" and then walk away. It sounds simple but can be surprisingly upsetting to a person trying to tease.

Pretending you can't remember a teaser's name was another of my mom's approved tactics. "Just look puzzled when they look at you," she'd say. "Ask, 'Who are you? What was your name again? Wasn't it Linda? Or was it Belinda? I'm sorry. I can't remember. What did you say? I didn't hear that, Louise.'" It's essential to use names that resemble the teaser's or at least start with the same letter.

One of the more ingenious counterattacks mentioned by psychologist Dr. Dorothea Ross is a strategy suggested by one of the children who worked through her teasing program. The idea is to ask a teaser before he or she says anything at all, "What's it going to be today?" and rattle off a list of taunts that the person has used in the past, then actually offer to help think up some brand-new ones. ❑

AGE FACTOR

❖ Even at young ages kids can use comebacks, but they work best when kids are at least 8 years of age. The reason? Most comebacks, especially counterattacks, depend on having an advanced sense of language and humor that younger kids often don't understand.

Kid Tactics 4: Act It Out First

Even if they come up with ideas for behaving differently when another child is mean to them, most kids find it very difficult to change the way they react to a situation. As we all know, it's one thing to think of a new way of doing something; it's another to follow through and do it. Emotion clouds our good intentions when we're scared, our tempers flare, or our feelings are hurt, and all of us—adults included—tend to forget what we've planned and to respond the way we always have.

Through acting out situations with you, kids can practice standing up straight and looking others in the eye. They can also try out solutions like humorous comebacks or telling someone how they feel over and over until they can do it with confidence.

Take small steps first. When seven-year-old Billy was being bothered on the bus, he and his dad started by playing teasing games in which they both tried to think of the silliest things they could say to each other. As Billy felt more at ease, they developed skits of real situations that Billy reported, concentrating first on not reacting and looking cool. Only later did they add in as many different rejoinders as they could think of for Billy to use the next time someone bothered him.

▶ PARENT TIPS

When you help your child practice:

▶ Show your child how you talk to yourself to stay calm and not react.

▶ When you're acting your child's part against a mean kid, don't do everything perfectly at first. Say, "Oops! I forgot to look you in the eye. Let's try again." Then gradually improve. That way kids are more willing to take the risk of trying themselves.

▶ In the beginning have your child act as a critic. Use some good and not so good nonverbal behaviors and have your child tell you how you should have reacted.

▶ Use a full-length mirror so kids can see their stance and facial expressions.

▶ Show kids how to break eye contact to end an encounter with a bully.

▶ Give praise at each step. If a child is shy, young, or being harassed daily, it may take a while before he is confident enough to use what he's learning.

How to help your child act it out

Scene: Most days Steve has trouble with Nathan, a boy in his third-grade class. On the playground Nathan grabs Steve's baseball hat at the beginning of recess, tosses it in the air and sometimes to a friend, pretends to give it back, and then laughs and jerks it away. When Steve gets upset, Nathan makes fun of him. Steve gives up the hat and feels terrible when he retrieves it, dirty and smushed, from the sandbox, just as the bell rings. ❏

1 Talk about ideas.

2 Write a script.

3 Think about how you look.
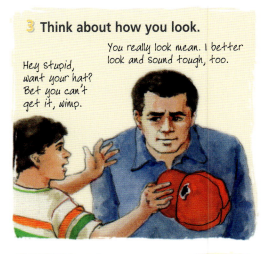

4 Try out your script.
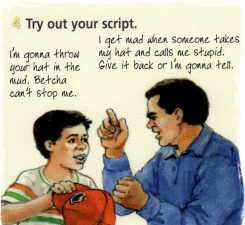

5 Take turns playing parts.

6 Try your script in front of an audience.

Kid Tactics 5: Use The Power Of Friendship

In the sixth grade of a small elementary school, there was a powerful bully named Robert, also the handsomest and smartest boy in the class. While he never beat anyone up, he would carefully select one boy at a time to harass and dump on for several weeks with razor-sharp, withering remarks and mean looks.

As so often happens, the rest of the boys in the class, afraid of being singled out themselves, not only didn't protest but went along, excluding Robert's unfortunate victim so they could stay on Robert's "good" side. First the victim was Ned; several weeks later he was back in favor and then it was Alan, followed by Jack, and then Aaron.

That's when Isaac decided to do something. Aaron had been his best friend since the first grade, and besides, Isaac could see his own turn to be dumped on was coming around soon. So with the encouragement of his dad, he persuaded all the boys in the class to band together against Robert. "He's going to pick on every one of us eventually," Isaac pointed out to them. "But if we all stand up to him at the same time, he won't be able to do it to any of us."

When they all confronted Robert together, of course, he had no choice but to back down and change.

Presenting a united front with friends is one of several ways kids can learn to use friendship to stop others from teasing, rejecting, harassing, and bullying them.

ASK THE EXPERTS

• **According to Dr. Ronald Slaby, a psychologist at Harvard University and the Education Development Center, even one child on the side of a victim can shift the power balance enough to prevent a bully's attack or change the course of a bully's actions.**

Stick with friends

Bullies are most likely to act aggressively with kids who are alone because it's easier. Just as a coyote goes after the lamb that's separated from the flock, so, too, bullies target kids who are isolated because they don't have anyone to back them up. The advice one dad gave his son, "Stick with your friends when the bully is around," is correct. If your child plays with a few buddies on the playground, eats lunch with them, and walks to and from school with them, chances are no one will bother him. Even if someone does, it will be easier for your child to stand up for himself with friends to talk to and support him.

Sometimes, though, a bully can isolate a child over time. That's what happened to Gary, who was just getting to know kids at his new school when another boy started harassing him. The kids Gary was hanging out with were intimidated by this bully and drifted away. His parents helped him find ways to establish stronger friendships so that he wouldn't be as vulnerable.

Develop friendship skills

Children like Gary may need help finding friends. Developing strong skills in music, a sport, or another activity is one way friendless children can become accepted into a group, according to Dr. Robert Cairns, a psychologist at the University of North Carolina who has studied kids'

social networks. Gary's dad signed him up for group drum lessons and coached him in soccer on weekends so he'd be seen as an important member of the team. Parents of younger children can help them set up playdates with classmates after school.

Other children are alone because they don't know how to make and keep friends or are shy and timid. They need coaching and practice in friendship skills such as how to approach and join a group of kids, how to negotiate and share, how to be agreeable, and how to compliment others (see pages 81-83).

Ask for help

If your child is one of those children who is mostly alone by choice, be sure he or she feels comfortable asking friends for help if someone starts trouble, a strategy kids with lots of friends use. At our town playground I've noticed two six-year-olds regularly rounding up a group before confronting one boy and telling him, "Stop hitting." Many kids, even siblings, are much more altruistic and protective than we give them credit for.

Adults know that a united front is more powerful than just one individual, but kids are just beginning to learn that. We can urge them to band with their friends in the face of mean behavior, as Isaac did. This is one of the few tactics that has an effect on the sexual teasing in middle schools. ❑

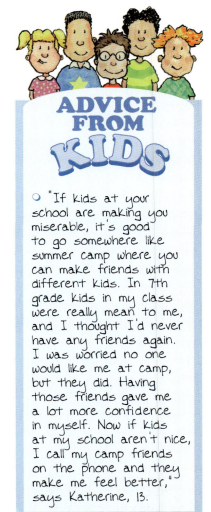

ADVICE FROM KIDS

○ "If kids at your school are making you miserable, it's good to go somewhere like summer camp where you can make friends with different kids. In 7th grade kids in my class were really mean to me, and I thought I'd never have any friends again. I was worried no one would like me at camp, but they did. Having those friends gave me a lot more confidence in myself. Now if kids at my school aren't nice, I call my camp friends on the phone and they make me feel better," says Katherine, 13.

Kid Tactics 6: Get Help From An Adult

Let's face it: while there are many ways for children to cope with other kids' mean behavior themselves, these methods don't work in every situation. If other tactics haven't been successful or a bully is beating up your child, it's time for him or her to get help from an adult.

That's what Wendy, a third grader, finally decided. When a boy in her class grabbed cookies from her lunch tray, she ignored him. Then, a few days later, after he kept shoving her in the cafeteria line and pushed her into the wall, she sternly told him to stop it and leave her alone. But he didn't. The next day he threatened her in the hall just before lunch and demanded her lunch money.

She reported what had happened to the lunchroom teacher, who sent the boy to the principal. The boy had to give the money back, apologize, and eat at a special detention lunch table for two weeks. He didn't bother her again. Wendy was sorry she hadn't sought help sooner.

When to tell

Most of us assume our children know when they should ask an adult to help them, but in dealing with mean kids, they aren't always sure. When is asking for help tattling? Is being put down over and over until you're upset serious enough to involve an adult? Even when they're being physically bullied, most older kids turn to parents and teachers only as a last resort. Some don't want to be caught "ratting" on their peers; others have difficulty admitting they need help or are convinced it's their own fault—no one would hit them if they weren't nerds to begin with. Younger kids are used to adults saying, "Stand up for yourself," and frequently confuse tattling and telling.

What helps: be very specific about the kinds of situations kids can't fix themselves. Moira made a list with her children of when they should run away and get help from an adult immediately: if an older or bigger child hurt them physically, threatened them, or touched them inappropriately. She also told them, "Try to stop their teasing and name-calling yourself, but if you can't or someone does something that makes you feel unhappy or scared, don't wait. Tell me or your teacher, so we can help you stop it."

Who to tell

Who should kids tell? Parents, of course. In school, younger children usually go to their teachers, but school counselors recommend kids make a list of all the people at school they could go to, from the playground supervisor to the principal. Counselors advise students to think of this list as "a personal support network" of people they can turn to for help. Which ones would be most likely to listen and sympathize? If one

ASK THE EXPERTS

• **Dr. David Perry, a psychologist at Florida Atlantic University who has extensively studied victims of bullies, says: "It's important not to put all the responsibility for trying to stop a bully on children. The responsibility for curtailing attacks really lies with adults. For some children and in some situations, getting help from an adult is the only way."**

According to psychologist Dr. Nathaniel Floyd, who has worked with bullied kids, some vulnerable children may need practice in how to get an adult's attention and convince them the problem is serious. Instead of whining, for example, which teachers often dismiss, kids should use their assertiveness skills (see pages 56-57).

Other ways to get help

Drawing attention to yourself while the other child is being mean to you is a way to get help without having to ask for it. My mother helped my sister come up with the following technique when she was in kindergarten and was worried about an older boy who surreptitiously twisted the arms of kids at the hall drinking fountain. When he tried this on my sister, she yelled "Ow," as loudly as she could so a teacher in a nearby room would come over to see what was happening—and catch the culprit.

Often kids who are reluctant to report bullying don't use opportunities to get help. If a teacher comes up and asks, "Is anything wrong here?" while a bully is bothering a child, he or she should be honest about what's happening and not, as many kids do, deny there's a problem. One boy who was bothered on the playground wrote an anonymous note to the principal asking him to watch during recess, and the boys picking on him were caught. ❑

person brushes off a serious complaint, children should try someone else. Ask your child to report back and let you know what happens so you can intervene if necessary.

Does the school have a code about reporting mean behavior and bullying? Some have a specific teacher in charge of the complaints. Kids are most comfortable going to an adult at school for help if there is a process that guarantees anonymity.

When To Go To The School

Much of the mean behavior we hear about from our children takes place in the school's social hot spots—the playground, the cafeteria, the school bus stop, the halls, and the classroom. So it makes sense to approach a teacher or the principal if children can't solve a problem themselves. When it's bullying, report it to the school immediately. The longer bullying goes on, the harder it is to end. If your children are over eight years old, though, they'll probably beg you not to tell. Since they're terrified of appearing to be tattletales, make sure a teacher or principal will preserve your child's anonymity. No, you are not being pushy or overprotective by reporting it.

Start with the teacher

The first step, especially if your child is in elementary school, is just what you'd expect: consult with the teacher. When Jay complained that another fourth-grade boy was calling him a "loser" and telling other kids not to play with him, his worried parents, like most of us, wanted to know what his teacher had observed in the classroom, whether Jay was doing something to provoke the boy, what she could do about the mean behavior, and ways they could help Jay at home.

A conference is the best way to hammer out a plan of action, whether the problem is mean teasing by a classmate, a child who feels left out, or bullying by an older child. Classroom teachers can often devise simple but highly effective solutions. Jay's teacher scheduled a general discussion on teasing and classroom rules for the next class meeting and put Jay and the teaser in the same cooperative math group where Jay, a star student, would shine and the teaser would have to work with him and turn to him for help.

Check with the teacher regularly for a few weeks, though, to make sure she's following through on the plan. Once children are beyond second grade, some teachers don't take teasing problems seriously and expect children to be able to handle even difficult situations themselves.

A teacher's thoughtless actions or sarcastic remarks on a child's height, weight, or some other difference occasionally turn out to be the cause of the problem. Often the teacher isn't aware of the effect she is having. Francesca's second-grade teacher, for example, called attention to her habit of biting her fingernails so regularly that soon her classmates began teasing Francesca about it. Her annoyed parents met with the teacher and asked her to stop. When she didn't, they asked the principal to intervene, and eventually he moved Francesca to a different second-grade class.

Go to the guidance counselor or principal

Sometimes it's better to go directly to the principal or school counselor, especially if the problem is serious, your child is in middle school, or your child is being picked on by an older child. Bring a written record of incidents.

Most principals begin by verifying the story, either alerting teachers to watch or monitoring it themselves. Then, like principal Don McConkey of Fall City Elementary School in Washington State, they confront a mean child with what they've seen (thus absolving your child from the charge of tattling), ask the bully to role play the situation to understand how your child feels and write an apology, and warn of the consequences if this behavior continues.

Schools usually have a process they follow if it does continue: they consult with the mean child's parents, keep him after school, insist he talk with a counselor, and sometimes even call in a local police officer. But a good principal arranges help for your child, too, such as moving her locker to a different location, changing a class so she can avoid the mean kid, or sending her to the school counselor to improve her assertiveness, social skills, or self-esteem.

Sometimes, like teachers, the principal doesn't follow through as well as he or she should. Ask your child to tell you if things don't improve.

Check the school atmosphere

Is your child's school an orderly, caring place where teachers talk respectfully to students? Or is it hectic, noisy, and tense, with crowded halls and teachers who yell and make sarcastic remarks? Guess which one will have the most mean behavior among students.

Besides expecting the school to take quick action for an individual problem, we all want the school to create a safe and pleasant environment. To really reduce mean behavior among children, experts say, schools and teachers must be committed to fostering an atmosphere that actively discourages it. The essentials are clear rules and consequences about behavior, good supervision in places such as playgrounds where children of different ages gather, instruction in how to resolve conflicts, and rewards for kindness, caring, and including others in activities and groups.

At one school, recess times are staggered so that younger kids are not intimidated by older ones. A bullying program used in twelve South Carolina schools encourages bystanders to report bullies and help victims. Other schools teach lessons about empathy to make kids understand how mean behavior affects others.

If the meanness quotient at your child's school is too high, you may have to campaign actively to lower it. A survey of kids' complaints conducted by the PTA can make school officials more aware of how pervasive bullying is and inspire action.

The school-bus problem

Three-quarters of an hour in a cramped space, a driver who needs to pay attention to the road, and twenty-five kids of varying ages is a good recipe for those mean-kid problems some of us remember—grabbing hats, throwing spitballs, and tossing papers and books out the window. The trip to and from school makes some kids miserable. "Can't you drive me?" they plead.

A simple solution for my son—and many others—was sitting right behind the bus driver with a friend. If that and other kid tactics (see pages 54-65) don't work, alert the bus driver to the problem and ask the school for help. When the boy on my son's bus continued to taunt and trip kids despite warnings from the principal, he was barred from riding the bus.

But few schools take much responsibility for school-bus behavior. As a result, parents have tried everything from acting as volunteer bus supervisors to insisting on fixed seating arrangements so the younger kids could be in the front of the bus.

If the school doesn't respond

A surprising number of schools regularly brush aside complaints about kids' behavior. Often parents hear these excuses: "We can't follow your child around all day."

stop an eighth-grade boy from making sexual remarks and gestures to a seventh grader, her dad warned him to keep away from her or face charges, taking along his minister as a neutral witness. It worked.

If a group of parents band together and demand it, a principal is usually forced to take action. Chances are your child isn't the only one being bothered. Under pressure from a group of fifth-grade parents who were angry about several class bullies, the head of one private school expelled the ringleader.

In extreme cases, parents have convinced the superintendent to transfer their child to another school.

"You should get counseling for your child to find out why others are hitting him." "Teasing is a part of growing up."

In the meantime, your child may be suffering. If the school does nothing, experts advise parents to take more drastic steps. Some families have success with direct action. When the school did nothing to

If children are being hurt or threatened, sexually harassed, or if their possessions are being destroyed, experts advise parents to file a report with the local police. Parents have even sued the school when their child was bullied or sexually harassed—and won. Title IX of the 1992 Education Act requires schools to provide a "nonhostile environment" for students. ❑

When Siblings Pick On Each Other

Many parents secretly harbor the illusion that in other families children are not mean to one another. We're afraid that only our own children behave in such awful ways—pulling each other's hair, pinching and hitting until someone screams, delivering nasty remarks like "No one likes you because you stink" at the breakfast table. The truth is most parents could compile a list of their children's mean behavior to one another during one week that could easily fill a small notebook.

Why siblings pick on each other

Why don't brothers and sisters treat one another with more love and loyalty and less meanness? If you think back to your own childhood, you'll realize the answer is simple. All the feelings and problems that motivate kids to be mean to one another (see pages 17-21) are much more intense in families. When the family is composed of stepsiblings, these can be even more complicated and difficult.

As every parent has observed many, many times, jealousy, resentment, and competition abound among siblings. Kids are always convinced a brother or sister is receiving more attention or praise or love from their parents or getting some privilege or item that they are not. They all want to be the first, the best, the most loved. Being mean is a way of getting even.

Living together day in and day out is also a recipe for continual conflict. Our children have more to fight over than they do with their friends in school—who gets to pick the TV program, eat the last piece of cake, sit in the most comfortable chair in the family room, sleep on the best side of the bedroom they share, or go clothes shopping with Mom. In fact, children in a family have to share constantly, which translates into never-ending fights over possessions, territory, and their parents' attention. If they don't have creative ways of solving all these conflicts, the result is mean behavior.

Boredom on a Saturday afternoon can also lead to unmerciful teasing—it's some-

---

▶ PARENT TIPS

▶ "When there are complaints about teasing, I make the kids reverse their roles for 15 minutes," says Ellen, mother of 2 boys.

▶ "We keep 2 boxes in the kitchen. In one, the children put notes with complaints about mean behavior; in the other, they put notes about the nice things someone has done for them. At our family meeting each week, we read them all aloud. No one gets punished, but children get rewards if others have mentioned their nice behavior," advises Margaret, mother of 2 girls and a boy.

▶ "Once a month we have 'appreciation night.' All of us write down 2 very specific things we like about each person in our family and we read them aloud. The girls like to make posters for their rooms with all the comments they've received," says Warner, father of 3 girls.

thing to do when there's nothing else to do and usually highly entertaining and rewarding for the teaser! And just like adults, children who are angry at a teacher or frustrated with a friend express their anger or frustration by being mean to the closest person around—a sibling.

Siblings know how to hurt

Children in a family also know precisely what their brothers' and sisters' "hot buttons" are in ways that outsiders often don't. This intimacy means they can zero in on the very thing that will cause the most hurt feelings—for instance, saying, "You're such a moron," on just the afternoon that a sister came home with a bad report card.

Temperament sometimes makes a bigger difference than age in how siblings treat one another. If one of your children usually reacts with more drama than another, you can be sure that's the one who will be teased the most. It's not always the youngest: in one family of four boys, six-year-old Henry delights in calling only one of his older brothers "doo-doo head" because it's guaranteed to make him furious. The other two brothers, by contrast, just laugh loudly and reply, "doo-doo head yourself."

Henry loves exercising that power over his brother because he doesn't have very much power over him in any other way. No matter how hard Henry tries to be

included, his brother says, "Stop hanging around! You can't play with us." Unlike at school, rejection among siblings is almost always related to age. Older siblings are the ones who exclude, and younger ones are the pests who beg to join in.

Ways to reduce meanness

All the tactics children can use with mean kids at school (see pages 54-65)—problem solving, staying calm, ignoring, standing up for yourself, comebacks, and getting help—also work with siblings. In addition to helping kids learn to use these methods, parents can tackle underlying reasons for meanness at home.

One way is to make sure you have established clear, specific rules and consequences. My friend Mary Irene, whose two boys are six and nine, has a chart on the kitchen wall with three good ones:

- *No hitting. Use words.* If hitting starts, each boy goes to his room.
- *No name-calling or hurtful teasing.* Whoever breaks the rule must think of something to say that is kind and do the other's chores that day.
- *Treat others with kindness and respect.* Whoever does something particularly kind is praised and receives a small reward.

Another key is teaching children ways to negotiate with each other and come up with their own solutions to conflicts without resorting to being mean—and letting

ADVICE FROM KIDS

When younger siblings want to tag along or play:

○ "Sometimes I let my brother, who's 6, play with me and my friend for half an hour. When the timer rings he has to leave," says Alex, 10.

○ "If my older sisters play with me on Saturday morning, I don't argue about the TV shows they want on Saturday night," says Johanna, 8.

○ "My mom said I had to let my brother skateboard with me and my friends. It made me mad. I said I would take him one day a week but no more, and she said okay," says Eric, 11.

DID YOU KNOW ?

◆ Many parents tolerate nasty behavior in boys that they wouldn't tolerate in girls, especially when they reach middle-school age.

them do it without adult intervention. Many parents are surprised by how well this works, even when two children are not close in age. When children are successful in coming up with solutions, don't forget the praise.

We can also correct the ways we sometimes inadvertently encourage our children's mean behavior. For example, child devel-opment experts all agree that siblings are usually less jealous and resentful of each other when parents aren't continually comparing them with remarks such as: "Why can't you be polite the way your sister is?" or "Your brother never has trouble keeping his room neat!" We also forget just how much our children copy us, especially if we're doing something negative! If you put down others when you are stressed out, your children probably will, too.

When children have some space of their own and a few activities that are separate from those of their siblings, they're often better able to appreciate and be nice to each other. Even in a small house it's possible to find corners where each child can have some privacy.

But, warns one mother, "Set small goals in eliminating meanness. If you aim for total family harmony, you'll probably be disappointed."

When you have a bully and a victim

A common occurrence in many families is two siblings playing out the roles of the bully and the victim. An older brother viciously teases and hits a younger one, who cries, doesn't stand up for himself, and seems to be more vulnerable every day. The "bad" one is punished; the "pathetic" one is protected. According to Adele Faber and Elaine Mazlish, authors of *Siblings Without Rivalry,* the best thing you can do is to stop regarding them as a bully and a victim. Instead remind the older one of his ability to be kind. Help the younger one learn to "protect himself and demand respect." This works, but remember that some siblings need to be taught how to be assertive (see pages 56-57).

When to intervene and when not to

Since the mean child and his victim live in the same house, the victim usually tries to get a parent to intervene and punish. Take this example: "Mom, Molly is so mean! She spit on my new sweater! You have to do something about her!" Most parents find that trying to get to the bottom of every complaint is a trap. Instead, encourage the two children to find their own solution first. Intervene only if they've tried to work it out and can't or the same problem keeps coming up again and again. When you do step in, say experts, give all your attention first to the child who is hurt.

Naturally, though, you must intervene if one child is physically hurting the other or you can tell a situation is about to take a dangerous turn. Be sure rough play is mutual. When Cooper shouted, "Dad, Austin scratched my arm with the scissors! It's bleeding. Get him to stop!" his dad stepped in, separated the two, and later, after they'd calmed down, helped them talk about it.

Take a long-range view

Yet, despite the many ways siblings can be mean to each other, they can also be surprisingly quick to protect a brother or sister from others' meanness. When a boy at school started picking on Cooper, for example, his older brother Austin warned the boy to "leave my brother alone." ❑

ASK THE EXPERTS

● **According to the late Louise Bates Ames, a psychologist and child-care authority, parents sometimes over-identify with one child when it comes to mean behavior. If you were always picked on by an older brother, you're liable to see your daughter as "the poor darling" and your son as "the mean big brother." As Ames wrote in** *Questions Parents Ask,* **"If anything can cloud a clear evaluation of a present situation, it can be an over-identification with your own past."**

When Your Child Is The Mean One

There are two ways we usually find out that our children are being mean, and both are upsetting. One is the dreaded bad-news phone call from the teacher. "I think you should know what your son did at school today," the third-grade teacher said in a quiet but stern tone. "For a week or so he's been teasing a younger boy in the lunchroom, and today he actually kicked him. He spent most of lunch and recess in the principal's office. I think we should talk." The culprit was my son. I agreed. When I hung up, I felt terrible.

The other is observing or overhearing the meanness yourself, as Helen did one Saturday afternoon. In the kitchen, over frozen pizzas, her twelve-year-old daughter, Carol, and two of her friends were gossiping about another girl in their class that they didn't like and plotting some mean tricks. From the adjoining laundry room, Helen heard Carol say, "Tomorrow we'll invite Vanessa to meet us at the mall—but when she arrives, we won't be there! Then on Monday, we'll say, 'You must be really dumb to think we want to be with you!'" When they all laughed, her daughter loudest of all, Helen was horrified.

It's hard to accept that your own wonderful child is the one making someone else miserable, whether by kicking, cruel teasing, or hurtful tricks and whether the behavior is directed at schoolmates or siblings. It's easy to forget that all the reasons why other children are mean hold for our children, too (see pages 17-21). As parents, we have to take steps to curb it.

When should you intervene?

Helen, like many parents, was not sure what to do. Was her daughter's behavior just typical of girls in middle school? Even if it was, shouldn't she tell Carol exactly what she thought about it? In the end, Helen took her daughter aside and said, "I understand that you and your friends don't like Vanessa. I wonder if she did something to make you very hurt or angry. But what you're planning is cruel and unkind. You can't treat someone that way just because you don't like her or because you're angry or hurt."

Almost all experts would agree with Helen's decision. If you see or overhear your child being mean, they say, it's important to do something right away. Besides acknowledging the feeling that inspired the mean behavior, they suggest that parents, as Helen did, make clear that the behavior is unacceptable, and, in addition, offer alternative ways to express the same feeling. Perhaps Carol could have talked with her mother about what Vanessa had done.

If you catch your child in the act of being mean to another child, give comfort to that child first. Then suggest ways he can tell your child how the mean behavior makes him feel.

Sometimes it is better to let children get caught in their own web of friendship intrigues and learn the consequences of their mean behavior directly. But if your child is truly ostrasizing another, speak out. Kids learn how to treat others from us.

Speak with the teacher

A conference with the teacher is definitely in order if your child's mean behavior is at school, even if the teacher doesn't suggest one. Not only do you want to determine what triggered the behavior, but you also want to map out a coordinated plan with the teacher—or principal—to end it.

Before you go, though, get your child's view of what happened. My son claimed Lewis, the younger boy he'd kicked, was a terrible pest, following him everywhere at lunchtime and "bugging" him by repeating everything he said. I let him know I was on his side, and we'd work it out.

Specific questions can help you and the teacher discover a pattern. Is your child being mean to just one child or several? Does it happen in particular times and places? How often has the teacher spoken to your child about this behavior? Does it seem related to academic problems?

Work with the school

Any plan with the school should spell out three things: what's allowed, what's not, and the consequences. My son was not to

kick, hit, or tease Lewis, and if he did, he would eat lunch alone in the classroom. We also suggested that when Lewis was "bugging" him, he write down or tell Lewis exactly how he felt, tell Lewis firmly to stop, count to ten, or ask a teacher for help. Share such a plan with your child at a later meeting and get his ideas, too.

If the problem is more serious (your son has been endangering a child by throwing rocks at him, for example) or if your child is in middle school, the teacher or principal may want him present at the initial meeting and require him to sign a contract agreeing to the plan.

In either case, check in regularly with the school to monitor your child's

▶ PARENT TIPS

- ▶ "I keep a large cardboard box in the basement filled with small boxes and crumpled papers. I tell my older son, 'When you feel angry at your brother, get in the box, stomp down the papers, and say whatever you want to until you don't want to hit any more,'" says Irene, mother of 2 boys.

- ▶ "I realized my daughter teased her brother more right after two particular television shows. Now we have a rule that those programs are off limits," says Jane, mother of a boy and a girl.

- ▶ "Don't get angry at your child because you're embarrassed about his behavior at school and worried the teacher thinks you're a terrible parent! Make sure your child knows you think he's great. It's his behavior you don't like!" advises John, father of a boy.

progress—perhaps asking the teacher to send home a note at the end of each week.

Dealing with peer pressure

No matter what children's ages, peer pressure can encourage them to be mean in ways they probably wouldn't be alone. Most five- and six-year-olds tease and say mean things, but when two best friends this age gang up on others, they often get carried away, egging each other on in pushing, hitting, pinching, and tripping.

Rather than prohibit the friendship, use it. The parents of one such duo ended their bullying by asking the teacher to separate them at recess and tell them why. They also followed up with consequences at home—as long as the two didn't bully at school, they could play together on Saturday.

Similar problems often arise in middle school, when kids are trying to be part of a particular group. Your best bet is to allow children to keep their friends, but at the same time take a hard line about the behavior. Until you are convinced your child can say no the next time the friends want to do something mean, insist their time together be spent at your house and on outings supervised by you.

If your child is the bully

Most parents are taken completely by surprise if they're told that their child is a bully at school. But before you rush to his or her defense, as most parents do, hear what the school has to say and get as much information as you can about the incidents. Be sure it's bullying (see pages 28-31). Many young children who are impulsive go into overdrive when excited or angry, but don't have the malicious motives of a bully. You don't want the label to stick.

If your child is bullying others, get help from the school counselor or psychologist. Besides developing a strategy for handling the problem at school, he or she can help you look at what you're doing at home. Since bullies rarely outgrow this behavior without help from adults, it makes sense to start sooner rather than later.

Practice better behavior at home

Whatever your child's mean behavior at school, you can work to improve some part of it at home. For my son, as with many kids in elementary school, that meant figuring out ways he could control his temper—or, as we called it, anger patrol. With some practice he learned to notice when he was starting to get angry, calm himself down by imagining he was skiing down a hill, and think of a different way to handle the situation.

Sometimes children act mean because they don't know how to get what they want in any other way. Teaching them how to be assertive (see pages 56-57) gives

---

AGE FACTOR

❖ When children are 5 and 6 years of age, mean behavior is often simply immaturity. What you think is an insult or mean remark may simply be a fact to a young child.

❖ You also have to tell kids under 8 or 9 years old how others feel because they are too young to put themselves in others' shoes.

them appropriate ways to accomplish the same thing. Your child may need practice in being kinder and more sensitive to others' feelings (see pages 78-80). If your child teases, spend some time listing all the mean and nasty words you can think of, then discuss how they make people feel.

Regular routines and clear rules at home are essential in preventing children's mean behavior. Be specific about what's permitted and what's not. When children are mean to others, make the consequences a way to make up for being unkind. Then say, "Let's start over." ❑

Teach Kids How To Treat One Another

Sometimes our kids surprise us with a sudden and unexpected act of kindness to another child. Sam's dad noticed the new boy hovering at the edge of the ball-field looking awkward and uncomfortable. He was pleased and proud when his popular eight-year-old son interrupted what he was saying to his teammates and waved the new boy over. "Hey, come on," Sam said. "You're part of the team now, too!"

Later, his dad commended Sam for his kindness and pointed out how happy it made the new boy. "He was looking sad, like he was feeling left out," Sam said, "so I guess that's why I did it."

Children like Sam, who notice and care how others feel, are far less likely to be mean to others and far more likely to act in a kind way. They're also less likely to be the target of mean behavior and more likely to help and stand up for someone who is being victimized. These are powerful reasons to encourage your child to develop more empathy and kindness.

The importance of empathy

When children have empathy, they're sensitive to other kids' feelings, can see things from another child's point of view, and begin to grasp the effect their own actions might have on others. Kay teases Janie until she finally cries, but Ike thinks, "Janie will be unhappy if I make fun of her shoes, so I won't." As you can imagine, children with empathy find it easier to get along with others and are usually good at identifying their own feelings. This in turn makes them better at solving problems and at coming up with more options when dealing with mean kids.

How to foster empathy

The simplest way to encourage empathy in our children is to remind them of the other child's feelings every time they're mean to someone. "How do you think Jill feels when you pinch her?" Mimi asks her five-year-old daughter. "It hurts her. Now she feels upset and angry at you." Researchers have shown that when parents consistently react like Mimi, their children are kinder and more empathetic.

Here are three other empathy training techniques many parents use in everyday situations:

- *Help your children identify how they are feeling and empathize with them.*
- *Tell your children how what they do makes you feel.*

▶ PARENT TIPS

▶ "Our family plays a 'Secret Friend' game. We each draw a name from a hat and keep it secret. During the following week each person does kind things anonymously (like leaving a nice note on a pillow or doing a chore) for their 'secret friend,'" says Jane, mother of 3.

▶ "Last year we sponsored a child in a foreign country. Our children wrote letters, sent some of their toys, and even sent money they'd earned by doing chores for a neighbor. They felt so good about what they'd done," offers Richard, father of 2.

▶ "Each month everyone in our family, including parents, picks out one good deed to do for someone in our community. Our kids have taken flowers to a sick person, helped a younger child with homework, and cooked food for the local homeless shelter," says Connie, mother of 3.

- *Call your children's attention to other peoples' facial expressions in the mall, at a party, or even in a book, and ask your children to guess what they are feeling and why they might feel that way.*

Don't be surprised if developing empathy takes time. Some kids seem to intuit the feelings of others from an early age, but most edge slowly toward concern for others and have great difficulty applying their own feelings to their friends and family. We've all despaired over our children's self-centeredness, watching the daughter who was upset because she was left out of a sleepover turn around and thoughtlessly leave someone else out the next day.

AGE FACTOR

❖ Don't expect kids to have more empathy for others than they can at a particular age. Children's ability to understand other people's feelings does improve as they grow older, but sometimes it takes much parental effort and a long time for children to accept that the world doesn't revolve around them.

Children begin to develop empathy as early as age three or four, but only at ages ten to twelve does their ability to put themselves in someone else's shoes really take off—especially for those they think are like themselves.

Practice kindness

All children can benefit from more practice in the kindness department—even the ones who are usually sweet and kind. As a start, praise your child whenever you catch him treating others kindly, just as Sam's dad did. Approval and rewards for doing something right almost always make a much stronger impact on kids than our lectures about being mean.

We often assume that our children know how to be kind, but they don't. So give kids some ideas about ways they can help, comfort, befriend, and show affection to others, both friends and family. Some examples from parents:

"Your friend Laura has been sick all week. I'll bet she'd appreciate a phone call from you."

"You know so much about computers. Would you take some time to help your brother fix his?"

"It would be thoughtful of you to include Jonah in your party. I notice a lot of kids don't."

"Grandma is feeling sad. Why don't you bring her this cup of tea and say something nice to her to cheer her up!" In fact, researchers have found that when teachers encourage children to say nice things to each other, the children are more likely to do nice things for each other, too.

Like most adults, kids are more likely to be kind when they are happy and emotionally secure themselves.

Make your values clear

It's easy to forget that we teach children about empathy and kindness every day through our own example. If we treat our children and other people with kindness and generosity, they probably will, too—with a few nudges, family rules, and rewards. But if we don't, they won't. According to psychologist Dr. Ronald Slaby, children are much more likely to do something nice if they have seen others whom they respect and love do it first.

The values of kindness and caring aren't much evident in the world today, making it even more important for us to let our kids know exactly how important they are to us. When we take time to do good things for others and involve our children, we can also call their attention to how good it feels to perform simple acts of kindness for others. Through experience our children can learn that being nice feels better than being mean, and with time these good feelings will build. In the end, that will have more impact than a lecture. ❑

We all know adults who have trouble getting along with other people. Maybe they argue too much or come on too strong with their opinions or just don't seem interested in anyone but themselves. "He's certainly lacking in people skills," we say, or "She could use some pointers on how to behave with others."

Children can lack important social skills, too. And if they do, they may find themselves on the receiving end of other kids' meanness—being rejected, teased, or made fun of. The ages from five to thirteen are a crucial time for kids in learning how to make friends and how to get along with their peers. Though many kids pick up and absorb social skills informally, most need at least occasional reminders from, and practice with, us to learn them.

How to join a group

Whether kids are five or ten or thirteen, the process of trying to join a group is the same. Seven-year-old Robbie sees some boys playing ball at recess and wants to be in their game. Child development experts say that how he goes about trying to join in will determine whether he is accepted or rejected. The same is true for our kids.

What's the key? Going slow and being able to tune in to social cues. Typically, kids first hover cautiously at the edge of the group and watch the others for clues to what's going on. Then they try something tentative to show they catch on. Robbie, for example, started running around the way the others did, but only at the edge of the group, and he didn't try to grab the ball. He called a few remarks to the nearest boy, and eventually, when everyone seemed to accept his presence, a boy shouted, "Hey, Rob, catch!" Only after he'd thrown quite a few balls did Rob offer a suggestion about adding a new rule.

All children are rebuffed sometimes, even the most popular ones, but destined for rejection are kids who go in like gang-busters, argue about rules, and try to take control before checking out how others feel. A direct request like "Can I play, too?" rarely works with a group, but may with one child, as long as a child smiles and doesn't push too hard or talk too much.

Approaching the right group is important, too. The best bets: a single child, a group of four or more, kids who are generally friendly and welcoming, and those with similar interests to your child's.

How to be a friend

During the elementary- and middle-school years, kids learn the rules of friendship— how to make friends and how to keep them. Since everyone wants friends, these are important lessons to learn. Younger children have a simpler view of friendship than older ones do, but the old adage still applies: "To have a friend, be a friend."

Social Skills Kids Need

AGE FACTOR

❖ In kindergarten and 1st grade a friend is usually someone who will do what you want.

❖ By age 8 or 9 kids select friends on the basis of mutual interests and whether they are fun to be with. Their group alliances shift and change frequently.

❖ By age 12 or 13 kids choose a best friend of the same sex who is loyal and understands them, someone to whom they can confide feelings and on whom they can rely for advice. Their friendships are intense and exclusive.

Take ten-year-old Jenny, who is liked by everyone. She notices Ann's new red sweater and compliments her. When Tania talks about how sad she is because her dog is lost, Jenny listens and offers to help look for it. At lunch, she shares the chocolate cookies in her lunchbox with both of them. She laughs a lot and is fun to be with. Children like Jenny, who are kind and sensitive to what others are feeling, are most often chosen to be "best friends," according to one study of close friendships among ten- and eleven-year-olds.

Children who are good at friendship are also flexible and agreeable enough to shift gears when their friends want to do something else, take criticism and occasional rebuffs in stride, are not bossy, don't always insist everyone do things their way, and do not always run to the teacher.

Of course, they don't have to be perfect and act this way all the time. With boys, athletic prowess can often go a long way toward neutralizing bossiness, but it won't help if they run to the teacher or cheat in games. We can help our children practice complimenting, listening, sharing, being agreeable, and accepting criticism at home.

How to show loyalty, sensitivity, and tact

Tact and sensitivity are usually not our children's strong points. But by third or fourth grade, most understand how forgetting these things and being disloyal hurts a friendship. To most kids the three no-nos are: breaking a promise, as when a friend says she'll walk home with you and then goes off with someone else; revealing a secret you told her; and embarrassing you—maybe by jokingly telling the boy you like that you like him.

By junior high, what also counts in friendship is being willing to share personal facts and feelings and to let your friends disagree with you without assuming the friendship is over.

When they're trying to repair a friendship hurt by betrayal, children need sensitivity, tact, and loyalty to know when they've gone too far, when to apologize, and how to make amends. We can help them think through what happened, suggest options, and encourage them to keep a sense of humor.

How to resolve conflicts

This may be the most vital social skill for children to learn—and it's one bullies and victims don't have. As we all know, there are so many conflicts among kids from ages five to thirteen! What do you do when you disagree on the rules of a game or a boy won't stop calling you "goofball"?

Kids who can keep their tempers, don't arbitrarily insist on their own way, negotiate and accept reasonable compromises, and readily apologize have more friends, are less likely to be picked on, and are less likely to be mean. They know how to manage conflict so their friendships don't end just because they don't agree. By age seven or eight, kids expect others to be able to compromise—they don't like kids who act mean or make sarcastic remarks.

How to read and give social cues

We all count on certain kinds of social rules to let others know how we feel about them and to learn how they feel about us. These rules make our behavior predictable and put others at ease. Ariel knows Rachel is interested in her because she looks Ariel in the eye and smiles a lot when they are talking, asks questions in an animated way, and adds her own thoughts to the conversation. She listens carefully without interrupting—most of the time—and even stands in a way that conveys the message: "Ariel, that is so fantastic!" If Ariel frowns or looks upset, Rachel may ask herself, "Uh-oh. What did I say?"

Often children who are teased or rejected don't react in the usual social ways. Their problem may be easily corrected—remem-

bering to smile instead of looking like a grump—or may be more complex and extensive, in which case others will probably find them strange (see pages 37-38).

Reading social cues also includes intuiting other subtle signals, such as what your clothes and the way you talk say about you and understanding when kids are only play-fighting. ❑

Plan Ahead

Fact: it usually takes time before new children at a school are accepted, and during that time they are frequently the target of teasing. Children entering kindergarten or middle school are also the new kids at a school, and they, too, are often picked on by others who already have friends and a secure place.

Planning ways to minimize teasing in advance can make a new school a challenge instead of a threat. Not surprisingly, preparing children for any new situation makes them feel more at ease when they get there, and it's especially important for those who feel awkward and shy in new places. Since my husband, my son, and I each attended three different elementary schools, we feel we've had a fair amount of experience with this problem.

▶ PARENT TIPS

▶ "When we moved, we signed our son up for a summer camp program at his new school. By meeting a few classmates in advance, he started school with friends," says his mother, Judy.

▶ "Encourage kids to join a town sports team and to choose at least one extracurricular activity at school, even if they don't want to. These informal settings are quick ways for them to connect," suggests Jack, father of 3.

▶ "I volunteered to be the class mother, even though I have a full-time job, so I could get to know parents of my daughter's classmates and invite families over," says Bridget, mother of 2.

Why new kids are teased

New children are unknown and unfamiliar, may look, sound, and act different, and have no friends—all the things that inspire teasers. Just like other children who are alone without anyone to back them up, they're easy targets.

The groups that have been in the school for several years have a history together. If children in them feel insecure, they may not be very enthusiastic about someone new. They wonder: Will this new kid change who likes whom? Will he take away my best friend? Will he fit in? The school atmosphere can make a big difference. Some schools, especially small ones, are insular and exclusive, others are more welcoming, friendly, and inclusive.

Kindergartners and first-year middle schoolers are targets because they're the youngest and most vulnerable and have the least social experience at the school.

Check out dress styles

New kids usually look, sound, and act different because dress codes and styles vary from school to school as do slang, hair styles, and customs. At one middle school, makeup is the norm in seventh grade; at another only the "bad" crowd wears it. In one third grade, all the boys wear jeans; in another they wear T-shirts and sweatpants. In one school girls have their ears pierced by age seven; at another few do before the age of ten. And the shoes that were acceptable in elementary school may no longer fly in middle school.

So, if you can, visit the school with your children before they start. That way they can check out how the kids dress and cut their hair. Then plan your new-clothes-for-school purchases accordingly. If one particular style or make of shoe or jeans seems to be popular, make sure you at least purchase that—if your kids want it. Some children are quite comfortable looking different from others.

Think positive

I sometimes think parents of children starting a new school tend to fall into two groups. One group is very worried about how their children will fit in and like their new school and whether they will have friends. Not surprisingly, these parents' anxieties are often picked up by their children, who then enter school feeling timid and fearful of what others might say or do to them—and as a result, don't cope as well.

The other group takes a more positive tack, assuming their children will be able to handle whatever comes their way in terms of teasing. This approach works the best. But being positive doesn't mean not preparing our children for the fact that it might be a challenge at first. When kids talk about and think about why others might tease in advance, they're better able to imagine what they might do. We can let them know that how they react initially to teasing will set the tone. If they can laugh it off, chances are it will end right there. Sometimes teasing is actually a sign of being accepted. It helps to encourage children to take a positive attitude and to assume the teasing is temporary. My dad counseled being friendly to everyone, smiling a lot, and not being too pushy. It works.

The best time to change schools

If possible, don't move in the middle of the year, especially if your child is older than eight. By then social alliances are usually in place and your child is likely to remain an outsider for much longer—even until the end of the year. Are there exceptions? Definitely. At one small school, kids in the fourth grade, who had known each other since nursery school, were totally bored with each other. Jonathan's arrival in early December was greeted with excitement, and everyone vied for his attention.

If another new child is entering the school at the same time, ask the principal whether he could put the two new children in the same class or homeroom.

A move that coincides with your child entering middle school is sometimes easier for kids because most middle schools draw students from several different elementary schools. As a result, many kids will be new to others. ❑

ADVICE FROM KIDS

To make friends at a new school:

○ "I made friends first with a girl who didn't seem part of a group," suggests Francie, 10.

○ "My mom and dad planned one really special activity, like going fishing, every weekend. I could invite one kid from my class to come. Everybody wanted to be my friend," explains Philip, 6.

○ "Try not to be shy, or kids will think you're snobby," says Tessa, 13.

○ "Tell the truth about what you did at your old school. Somebody will find out if you don't and then you're in for it," advises Fred, 13.

Does Your Child Need Professional Help?

Most of the problems children have with mean kids can be solved with help from parents or from a combination of parents and the school. The same is true if your child is the one acting mean. But some problems are tougher to solve.

Patrick, a kindergartner, has been teased all year and now hates school.

Alma, an eleven-year-old, cries herself to sleep every night because she has no friends.

Don, who's thirteen, talks about how worthless he is because he was victimized by a bully for six months before the school finally expelled the boy.

These kinds of experiences can leave deep scars and cause enormous amounts of stress and unhappiness that may interfere with children's lives and their ability to grow and learn.

Ask yourself some questions

Since you know your child and the situation better than anyone else, ask yourself how long the problem has been going on, how much it seems to bother your child, and how much it interferes with his or her life. All kids feel miserable because a friend didn't play with them at one time or another or because someone called them a name. But usually this is transitory.

If your child has been suffering for a while and is continuing to suffer, if your child is always sad and depressed and doesn't want to go to school, if a teacher expresses serious concern, if your child is doing poorly academically, if your child seems to feel worthless and has battered self-esteem, think seriously about getting professional help.

Bullies, victims, and kids who don't fit in

Three groups of kids and their families always benefit from consulting a professional. Bullies do not outgrow their problem unless a professional helps both the bully and his or her family change what's going on at home. Victims of long-term bullying often require professional help to recover their self-esteem and to change their family's dynamic of overprotection.

Psychologists also believe that children who have no friends at all clearly need professional help so they can overcome the problems preventing them from connecting with others. If part of the reason they are socially isolated is an inability to read social cues, they'll need to work with a professional for a time to learn how.

What kind of help

The guidance counselor or school counselor may be sufficient if the problem isn't too severe, but long-term bullies and victims are helped most by a psychologist or psychiatrist who has some experience with children with similar problems. ❏

YEAR BY YEAR

What To Expect At Different Ages

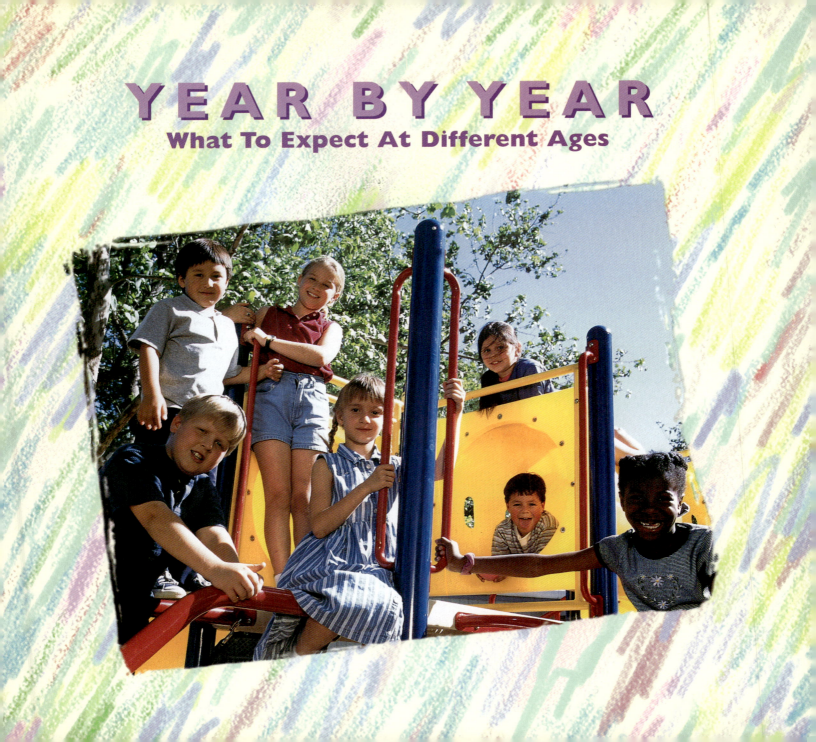

What To Expect At Different Ages— Friendship, Social Skills, & Being Mean

Between the ages of five and thirteen, relationships with other children are a central ingredient in our kids' lives, and these experiences influence their feelings of self-worth into adolescence and beyond.

● *What all ages have in common.* They want friends and find rejection painful. Pairs of friends tend to be the same age, sex, size, level of intelligence, and have the same degree of physical maturity. At all ages, children know many ways to be mean, and some on the receiving end respond to such behavior more effectively than others. Those who don't know how or lag behind in social skills may continue to be targets—a child rejected at six may still be rejected at eleven.

● *What changes with age.* As children grow, how they regard friendship changes. So do their abilities in compromising, controlling anger, solving conflicts, and looking at situations from another's point of view. Even the ways they are mean change. The evolution is more like a continuum than a smooth upward progression with clear age markers. One seven-year-old may have more skill at compromising than a ten-year-old; another may still hit like a five-year-old.

Ages 5 to 7

● *Friendship and social skills.* Children are learning fundamentals of friendship, and patterns of relating to others are being set in place. Most now prefer same-sex playmates. Much of kindergarten is about getting along, but five- and six-year-olds are still very self-centered, choosing playmates who go along with what they want. Self-interest and fear of punishment still motivate their behavior: "If I'm nice, he'll be nice" or "Mom will kill me if I tease my brother."

As kids try to feel confident in school, many are very upset by teasing and bewildered by rejection. Only at the end of this stage do they begin to see another's point of view, and they forget easily when they're feeling competitive or get into a conflict.

● *Ways of being mean.* About fifty percent of kindergartners experience teasing, name-calling, and mean tricks from others, but if they stand up for themselves, it stops. Hitting is subsiding, but in first and second grade popular boys often bully to establish themselves as leaders. Groups often gang up on others; in threesomes two kids may reject the third because they don't know how to play with more than one at a time. A common response when a friend won't do what a child wants is rejection— "If you don't do what I say, I won't be your friend." Some children habitually give in. Typical conflicts are over toys, who goes first, and wanting their own way.

● *Best solutions.* Separate kids, insist they do something else, provide supervision, and have a child "undo" meanness by doing something nice. Having clear rules and enforcing consequences are important, because kids still look to adult authority figures—or a bigger child, even a bully—to tell them what's right and wrong. They need to talk through a problem-solving strategy out loud.

Ages 7 to 10

● *Friendship and social skills.* Children go from seeing themselves at the center of the world to being able to infer others' intentions and feelings and to show empathy. They pick friends who share their interests instead of whoever is handy, and have a more mature understanding of how friends should treat one another. But everything is still quid pro quo—"I'll do something for you, if you do something for me." Gossip is one way they exchange information on what makes a good friend. By the age of eight they have relationships in which both share. By ages nine and ten, the peer group has become highly important, a laboratory in which to practice their growing skills.

Networks of loose friendships, clubs with officers, and games with rules characterize play. Children spend much time arguing about rules and roles, and those who are good at resolving conflicts without fighting are the most popular. To solve conflicts they rely on persuasion ("It'll be fun . . . you'll like it"), taking turns, and bartering ("I'll do it if you'll let me be on the team"). Most boys have more self-control, but play-fighting as a social activity continues until about age ten.

● *Ways of being mean.* Kids are now more likely to be angry at those who intended to hurt or be mean. At seven, teasing tends to be physical or name-calling; later bossiness, mean gossip and rumor-mongering, putting others down, and excluding are also rife, especially after age eight. One cause for rejection is not playing by the rules. Seven- and eight-year-olds find it particularly difficult to accept being excluded and blame themselves. The jealousy, "bossing," and intrigue that typify girls' friendships can shift daily and cause many hurt and confused feelings. Many kids still need help dealing with teasing, but teachers often don't take it seriously when kids are older than seven. Kids who still hit at age nine have become bullies—hitting becomes increasingly hostile—and without help their bullying is likely to continue.

● *Best solutions.* With conflicts, help kids work on problem solving and negotiating; with put-downs, tell children, "Please say something positive or leave the room," or insist they offer others three build-ups every time they use one put-down. For kids who are feeling left out, show them strategies for inviting friends to do things.

Ages 10 to 13

● *Friendship and social skills.* Children are beginning to understand complex and contradictory emotions. They have strong expectations for friendship and are often disappointed. Friends share secrets, personal ideas, and needs and these friendships become highly exclusive.

By fifth grade kids are beginning to develop more consideration of others and a greater ability to take another point of view; this ability grows as they develop the capacity for abstract thought. Having a best friend is very important from the ages of ten to twelve, and by then children view friendship as a relationship that grows over a period of time between two people who have mutual interests, personalities that mesh, and loyalty to one another. Friends are beginning to be able to weather differences and conflicts, but in seventh and eighth grade, friendships may end because kids develop physically and emotionally at different rates. Some children become highly upset when this happens.

In fifth and sixth grades, cliques form, and who's in, who's out, conformity, and peer pressure are at their height. Sports are often a qualification for boys' groups, and boys who aren't sports-minded may have trouble. Compromise is a skill that can be taught and used to solve problems. By ages twelve and thirteen, many kids begin to develop their own beliefs and values, as in "I shouldn't be mean."

● *Ways of being mean.* Teasing, bossiness, put-downs, betraying friendships, and being left out are very common. Teasing is nastier and more cutting than at younger ages. Targets are often early-developing girls in fifth and sixth grades, boys and girls who are smart, boys who are regarded as "sissies," and, in seventh and eighth grades, late-developing and short boys. Boys try to embarrass each other; girls spread rumors. Seventh- and eighth-grade girls and some boys are the targets of sexual teasing that can verge on harassment. By the end of eighth grade, however, most children have learned how to withstand and deflect teasing and name-calling. As for bullies, boys in the first year of middle school are often targets of older boys.

● *Best solutions.* Children rarely ask for help with teasing or bullying, even if it's hurtful, so watch for clues that it's going on. Expect your child to be unhappy and feel left out at least some of the time as part of the transition to adolescence. Help kids understand why a friendship ended so they can look for more satisfactory friends in the future. Make sure girls know they can say "hands off." In solving conflicts, focus on empathy, talking things out, and being assertive. Help kids find a group with similar interests and realize that to them wearing the "right" clothing is very important. ❑

WE RECOMMEND

Books, Videos, & School Programs

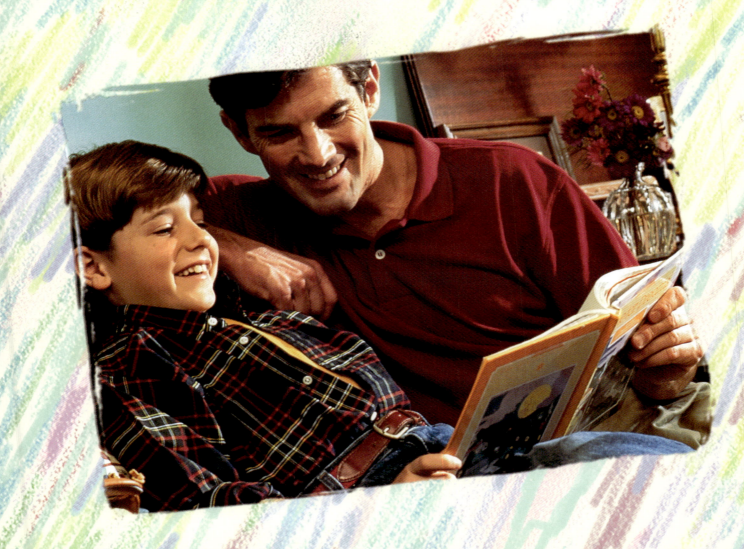

BOOKS

For Kids in Kindergarten-3rd Grade

THE BERENSTAIN BEARS AND THE BULLY
by Stan and Jan Berenstain (Random House, 1993)

When a tough new cub beats up Sister Bear, Brother Bear coaches her in self-defense methods that she ends up using when avoidance doesn't work. Other good titles in this series are: *The Berenstain Bears and Too Much Teasing* (1995), in which Brother Bear comes to understand why Sister Bear gets so mad after he's taunted at school; and *The Berenstain Bears and the In-Crowd* (1989) and *The Berenstain Bears and the Trouble with Friends* (1986), which are about friendship problems.

ARTHUR'S APRIL FOOL
by Marc T. Brown (Little, Brown, 1983)

Oversized Binky Barnes calls lovable Arthur a pipsqueak and threatens to punch him out. Arthur is so worried that he can't keep his mind on his performance of magic tricks for a school assembly. But when Binky volunteers on stage, Arthur devises a hilarious solution.

WILLY THE WIMP
by Anthony Browne (Knopf, 1989)

Willy is polite and gentle—even when the suburban gorilla gang calls him Willy the Wimp, a name he hates. Through a "Don't be a wimp" ad in a comic book, he learns to exercise, goes on a diet, and takes up body-building. His new strength proves useful in protecting his friend Millie from bullies—but doesn't change the kind of person he is.

HOW TO LOSE ALL YOUR FRIENDS
by Nancy Carlson (Viking Penguin, 1994)

With colorful pictures and tongue-in-cheek humor, Carlson pokes fun at bullies, grumps, whiners, poor sports, and other kids who alienate others.

LOUDMOUTH GEORGE AND THE SIXTH GRADE BULLY
by Nancy Carlson (Lerner, 1994)

Another winner from this author! George's friend Harriet helps him thwart a bully who has been stealing his lunch. The book shows how important a friend can be in fighting off a bully.

HOW TO BE COOL IN THE THIRD GRADE
by Betsy Duffey (Puffin, 1993)

Robbie plans to be cool this year by wearing plain white underwear and jeans and walking to the bus alone. But Bo Haney spreads a rumor that Robbie is wearing underwear with superheroes on it.

THE RAT AND THE TIGER
by Keiko Kasza (G. P. Putnam, 1993)

In Rat and Tiger's friendship, Tiger always gets the bigger piece and the most desired part. Rat, who is much smaller, finally has to stand up for himself.

BEST FRIENDS
by Steven Kellogg (Dial Books, 1986)

Compromise, sharing, trying to be accepted, losing a friend, and other themes of friendship are charmingly portrayed in this picture book.

KING OF THE PLAYGROUND
by Phyllis R. Naylor (Simon & Schuster, 1991)

The bully in the story is Sammy, and Kevin avoids him by staying off the swings and monkey bars when Sammy declares himself "king" of each one. But he doesn't let Sammy take over the sandbox.

DINOSAUR FRIGHT
by Colin Threadgall (William Morrow, 1993)

When bullying brachiosaurs invade the territory of smaller dinosaurs, a little nanosaur devises a clever plan.

I'LL FIX ANTHONY
by Judith Viorst (Simon & Schuster, 1969)

A younger brother imagines all sorts of funny ways he can take revenge on his mean brother, Anthony.

THE HATING BOOK
by Charlotte Zolotow (HarperCollins, 1969)

A beloved classic about a little girl who got up her courage to ask her friend why they were being so mean to one another.

For Kids in 4th-8th Grade

BULLY ON THE BUS
by Carl Bosch (Parenting Press, 1988)

In this excellent story, kids can choose one of several options for dealing with a bully on the school bus, then read on to discover the outcome. When they've read them all they'll know which works best.

I AM NOT A SHORT ADULT
by Marilyn Burns (Little, Brown, 1977)

This nonfiction book talks about deciding what kind of kid you want to be and has an excellent section on what your tone of voice, body language, and facial expression say about you. Definitely not a preachy book, it is written with humor and real knowledge of what matters to kids in fourth, fifth, and sixth grades.

WHAT A WIMP!
by Carol Carrick (Clarion, 1988)

Barney, a new fourth-grade kid, is set upon by two older boys who take his sled. One keeps harassing him on his way home from school. When he decides just to let the bully beat him up, the bully doesn't take him up on it. This is particularly appropriate for kids going to a new school.

LORD OF THE FLIES
by William Golding (Berkley Publishing Group, 1959)

This story of a group of British boys marooned on an island and how they treat one another is a classic, but most appropriate for more mature eighth graders.

THE SECRET LIFE OF HUBIE HARTZEL
by Susan Rowan Masters (Lippincott, 1990)

A bully is just one of Hubie Hartzel's problems in fifth grade—the others are a weight problem, schoolwork, and a sick cat. Hubie's father is against fighting the bully, but offers other ways to cope.

RELUCTANTLY ALICE
by Phyllis R. Naylor (Atheneum, 1991)

A bully and her friends gang up on another seventh-grade girl, making fun of her in class, throwing food at her in the cafeteria, and tripping her in the hall. But after the girl chooses to interview the bully for a class project and they come to know one another, the bullying stops.

WENDY & THE BULLIES
by Nancy K. Robinson (Scholastic, 1991)

Wendy and her friend maintain a command post in Wendy's basement, with a map of bully hangouts and a notebook of incidents and names. Good for both boys and girls, this book clarifies how bullies operate and offers a variety of excellent strategies for dealing with them—from a kid's perspective.

JOSHUA T. BATES TAKES CHARGE
by Susan Shreve (Knopf, 1993)

Fifth-grader Joshua Bates's biggest worry is being left out. But being "in" depends on whether Tommy Wilhelm and his friends label you a nerd as they do a new kid. Joshua doesn't want to get involved, but finally does at the prodding of his parents.

THE SHORTY SOCIETY
by Sheri Cooper Sinykin (Puffin, 1994)

Three short boys in the seventh grade, tired of being called shrimp and squirt, form the Shorty Society. But their revenge eventually gets out of hand and they start resembling the bullies.

THE BULLY OF BARKHAM STREET
by Mary Stolz (HarperCollins, 1985)

This story, one of a series of books about Barkham Street, is a good one, painting a vivid picture of a bully through the main character, the oldest and biggest boy in the sixth grade.

STICK BOY
by Joan T. Zeier (Atheneum, 1993)

During sixth grade, skinny Eric shoots up seven inches and becomes a misfit and the victim of the class bully.

For Parents

TEACHING YOUR CHILD THE LANGUAGE OF SOCIAL SUCCESS
by Marshall P. Duke, Stephen Nowicki, Jr., & Elisabeth A. Martin (Peachtree Books, 1996)

This easy-to-use guide by two psychologists and an educator explains how posture, facial expressions, tone of voice, and other nonverbal communication matter in children's relationships with other kids. It includes ways to help kids improve their nonverbal skills.

SIBLINGS WITHOUT RIVALRY
by Adele Faber & Elaine Mazlish (Avon, 1987)

Among the sibling issues this helpful book tackles are how to handle the teasing, name-calling, put-downs, hitting, bullying, and other mean behavior so common among siblings. The authors convey practical solutions through stories of real family problems brought up in their workshops.

Emotional Intelligence
by Daniel Goleman (Bantam, 1995)

This fascinating bestseller discusses the importance of empathy, social deftness, and other forms of "emotional intelligence" for success in life. It includes much information about how children develop these skills.

Playground Politics:
Understanding the Emotional Life of Your School-Age Child
by Stanley I. Greenspan, M.D.
(Addison-Wesley, 1993)

Greenspan, a psychiatrist and authority on child development, describes stages of emotional development in children from the ages of five to twelve. The first three chapters explore the rivalries, aggressiveness, and rejections that characterize kids' relationships with their classmates and offer parents fine advice on handling it all.

Bullying at School:
What We Know and What We Can Do
by Dan Olweus (Blackwell, 1993)

This psychologist, the world's leading authority on the topic, gives good practical advice on how to stop bullying in schools.

You Can't Say You Can't Play
by Vivian Gussin Paley
(Harvard University Press, 1992)

In this movingly written book, Paley, a kindergarten teacher at the University of Chicago Lab School (and a MacArthur fellow) describes her year-long experiment in the classroom to solve an issue most kids face at one point or another: feeling left out. It offers insights into why kids exclude and are excluded and how to help them with their feelings. Her new rule, "You can't say you can't play," changes what goes on in the classroom for the better, and kids begin to develop real sensitivity to the feelings of others.

Childhood Bullying and Teasing
by Dorothea M. Ross, Ph.D.
(American Counseling Association, 1996; order through ACA at 800/422-2648)

The most comprehensive overview of bullying and teasing, this book by a psychologist reviews current theory and offers extensive practical solutions, including a section on what schools can and should do. Ross has worked with many cancer patients who are teased when they return to school. Parents will find much of use in this book, particularly if their child is being bullied. An essential reference for guidance counselors and principals.

Bringing Up a Moral Child:
A New Approach to Teaching Your Child to Be Kind, Just, and Responsible
by Michael Schulman and Eva Mekler
(Doubleday, 1994)

Practical, inspiring, and sensible, this book by two psychologists offers many ways for parents to foster personal moral standards in their children from birth through adolescence, and to teach empathy, kindness, fairness, and much more.

VIDEOS

CLUELESS

In this movie set in a Beverly Hills high school, cliques, rejection, what it means to be a good friend, and much more are illustrated with humor through the adventures of Cher and her friends. In the end, good values triumph. It's most appropriate for sixth through eighth graders.

GOOSEBUMPS: THE HAUNTED MASK

To get back at some boys who've teased her, eleven-year-old Carly wears a Halloween mask with terrifying powers. The moral of the spooky story: teasing can be dangerous. For fourth graders and up.

KIDS FOR CHARACTER (LYRICK STUDIOS)

Favorite characters from kids' TV programs explain about caring, respect, and more for kids ages five to nine. It's entertaining, not at all preachy or silly.

LITTLE GIANTS

A group of kids labeled wimps and losers, coached by Rick Moranis, triumph in the Peewee State Championship football game against a team coached by Moranis's older brother, who is a bully and former football hero. For third graders and up.

MATILDA

Super-smart, six-year-old Matilda, misunderstood by her parents, wins out over a very mean principal with the help of a brave best friend. For ages eight and up.

STAND BY ME

Friendship is the theme of this highly-rated coming-of-age drama of four twelve-year-old boys who take off on a two-day trek in search of a missing teenager's dead body. Though based on a story by Stephen King, it's no horror movie. Expect the put-downs, teasing, and other behavior typical of boys this age. The "R"-rating is for profanity, kids shown smoking, and a view of a dead body. For seventh graders and up.

SCHOOL PROGRAMS

BULLY-PROOFING YOUR SCHOOL

by Carla Garrity, Katherine Gens, William Porter, Nancy Sager, and Cam Short-Camilli (Sopris West, 1994-1996; tel. 303/651-2829)

A comprehensive curriculum for grades one through six devised by several child psychologists, it includes training for teachers, instruction for students on what to do about bullying, and special lessons for use with victims and bullies.

SECOND STEP

by K. Beland (Committee for Children, Seattle, tel. 800/634-4449).

This excellent, extensively-tested curriculum teaches empathy, problem solving, behavioral skills such as how to join an activity, and how to manage angry feelings. Separate programs are available for different age groups, from preschool through eighth grade. ❑